The Free Earth Guide to Gardening

...is the catalog of catalogs for the indoor gardener who is tired of spending exorbitant amounts of money on pots, seeds, and plants, and for the outdoor gardener who has a small plot of land and wants a beautiful, abundant garden without going broke.

Jack Kramer is the well-known horticultural expert and gardening author. He has written more than 32 gardening books, including *Gardens under Glass: The Miniature Greenhouse in a Bottle, Bowl or Dish; Hanging Gardens; The Natural Way to Pest-Free Gardening;* and *One Thousand Beautiful House Plants & How to Grow Them.* Mr. Kramer has also written articles for such nationally known magazines as *House Beautiful, House & Garden, Family Circle, Woman's Day,* and *Architectural Digest.*

A *Better Homes & Gardens* Book Club Alternate Selection

THE FREE EARTH GUIDE TO GARDENING

THE FREE EARTH GUIDE TO GARDENING

Jack Kramer

PINNACLE BOOKS · NEW YORK CITY

I wish to thank the following people for the illustrations in
this book:

Kevin Haapala, chapter openings
Charles Hoeppner, pages 18 and 151
Houlgate David Davenport, page 163
James Carew for all other illustrations

Much of the material in Chapter 5 was compiled from the
1971 Directory of American Horticulture handbook issued by
the American Horticultural Society, Mount Vernon, Virginia.

THE FREE EARTH GUIDE TO GARDENING

Copyright © 1974 by Jack Kramer

A Pinnacle Books edition, published by special arrangement
with the Walker Publishing Company, Inc.

ISBN: 0-523-00567-9

First printing, March 1974

Printed in the United States of America

PINNACLE BOOKS, INC.
275 Madison Avenue
New York, N.Y. 10016

CONTENTS

AUTHOR'S NOTE

Garden books come and go; many are written each year. In general, they all tell you how to garden in one way or another. Yet with all these volumes there has been no single book that explored what most people want to know about gardening such as: where to buy plants, where to see plants and gardens, where to get helpful (and free) information about plants, and the various horticultural societies and organizations that offer a wealth of plant knowledge. This book fills that gap. In essence it is a consumer's guide for getting the most for the least.

I believe it is a necessary book at this time when we are bombarded by advertisers to buy this or that gardening product. It is indeed difficult to evaluate all these claims and testimonials to better gardening by using all these products. It boggles the mind of an experienced gardener, and it may frighten off the would-be gardener.

This book is based on my twenty years' experience in finding sources for plants, buying the right ones, getting information from free (or almost free) government sources and accumulating other tidbits of knowledge I have picked up along the way. It is *your book* too if you want to garden inexpensively. THE FREE EARTH GUIDE TO GARDENING can be used as a supplemental aid to other garden books, or by itself it can put you on the right road to good gardening without going broke.

JACK KRAMER

THE
FREE EARTH
GUIDE
TO
GARDENING

Chapter 1

Kevin Hagopian '77

1
BE A SAVER

There are two different groups of people—those who save everything and those who discard everything. In these days with expensive prices on all items (plants included) you will be wise to join the first group, because collected seed and plant cuttings can in time become free plants. Not every seed and cutting will yield a gift from nature, but most will with some care.

You must know when to collect the free seed and when to take cuttings from plants, and then how to get them growing. After some know-how you may have more plants than you want without spending a cent! And even if you are all thumbs, you will still have plants in due time for your garden and your home. The odds are all in your favor. If you plant a

1. Along roadsides, wild plants offer a variety of free seeds to grow your own plants. Mother Nature will not miss a few seeds but plants should never be taken. (PHOTO BY MATTHEW BARR)

2. These wild plants will bear seed at proper seasonal times; patience is the key to success in collecting the gifts from nature. (PHOTO BY MATTHEW BARR)

dozen seeds, you may not get a dozen plants, but you will get a few. And if you start ten or fifteen cuttings, you invariably will get some that strike root.

Collecting seed and taking cuttings of plants— leaves too—does not harm the mother plant. And although it is not proper simply to pick and snip at random everywhere and anywhere, there are occasions when asking for a cutting from a friend's plant is quite in order; friends are generally more than willing to share their green wealth.

You can also buy seed in tidy packets ready for sowing. They are inexpensive, and you get many seeds for little money. Seeds of many different plants are available at nurseries or from mail-order sources.

FROM ROADSIDE PLANTS

Even city dwellers will occasionally venture into the country; this is when they should scout for seed. I never recommend taking whole plants from the wild (in most cases you cannot legally do this because most native plants are protected by law), but you can readily gather seed without harming the ecology. The trick is to recognize seed pods and know when they are mature for picking. This may involve several trips to the site, but it will give you the chance to get out into nature.

Seed should be gathered when ripe and before it deteriorates on the ground. The best time for seed collecting varies for each plant from place to place and season to season. Generally, the time to get the free harvest is when the first seeds begin to fall. Seeds of most plants can be collected about 30 days after the flowering period. When collecting, take a few leaves to help you identify the plant. Capsules and

3. Look for seed pods like this in the wilds to start your new plants. (PHOTO BY EMIL BARNICH, JR.)

4. Lunaria seeds in their capsules ready for harvest to become gratis plants for you. (PHOTO BY JACK BARNICH)

5. Open seed pods and plant seed or store in glass vials at cool temperatures for future use. (PHOTO BY JACK BARNICH)

6. Seed can also be purchased in tidy packets from several suppliers or at local nurseries. (PHOTO BY AUTHOR)

pods can be stripped from the stems. Crush out the seed by hand, or tap pods with a block of wood on a table. For seeds with fleshy coverings, soak seed in warm water for 30 minutes and then place seed in a mesh; scrub through to get the seed.

Of course, it takes time to start seed, grow seedlings, and nurture a plant to maturity, but getting something for nothing always involves some work.

FROM FRIENDS' PLANTS

Almost any gardener will share a cutting or seed of his favorite plant with you if you make it clear that

11

7. To take cuttings from plants, use a sharp knife and sever the top 2 to 3 inches of the shoots. (USDA PHOTO)

8. Holly cuttings: top row shows cuttings starting root growth. Bottom row shows cuttings when first taken. (USDA PHOTO)

you are really interested in growing the plant. A great many garden plants are rampant growers and must be trimmed annually to keep them in bounds; for example, in California, Sedums and ice plants grow so quickly that they must be curbed periodically. Most people trim the plants twice a year; that is an ideal time to appear and ask for some cuttings.

Once you get the reward, take it home and start it. If it is a house plant cutting, and you can not get to it immediately, simply put it in a jar of water. If it is a seed, and you want to save it for future planting, put it in a glass vial and store it in a cool, shady place. People who ask, receive, and then just throw away the gift are only defeating themselves. Besides, what a waste! From the smallest seed, from the most straggly cutting, beautiful plants grow.

HOW TO DO IT

Now that you have the seed, what do you do with it? Nature has a few tricks that you will have to learn in order to take advantage of the free bounty. First, some basics: New plants can be started from seed (sexually) or from cuttings and leaves (vegetatively). The process of starting new life is quite simple with seed. Sow the seed on a growing medium (sterilized soil or packaged mixes in a shallow container). For containers, use throw-aways such as milk cartons cut in half and aluminum trays that frozen rolls come in. (See Chapter 7.) Many garden ads implore you to buy special propagating cases or mini-greenhouses to really get seeds going, but don't do it—they cost money. Seed will grow as well in empty household containers.

Be sure the container you use for seed is at least 3 inches deep and has some drainage facilities. Punch tiny holes in the bottom of the container. Use standard growing mediums (sold in packages at nurseries): vermiculite, perlite, and sphagnum. If you use soil from the garden (free), you will have to sterilize it so weeds and bacteria do not interfere with the germination process. To sterilize soil, put it on a cookie sheet in an oven at 200°F. with the door open, and "cook" for an hour.

Sow seeds about 1/2 inch apart. Cover large and medium seed with a layer of dry mix, generally twice the thickness of the seed; merely scatter fine seed on top of the soil. Sprinkle the surface with water so the seed bed is uniformly moist but not soggy. Cover the bed with a Baggie or any household plastic. (Make a tent on sticks so the plastic does not stick to the soil.) Keep seed trays in warmth (average house temperatures) and out of sun but in bright light. Germination

1. select planter and punch holes in bottom for drainage

2. fill with 3″ growing medium

3. sow seed and sprinkle water lightly

4. secure poles in soil and place plastic bag over to maintain humidity

Planting Seeds

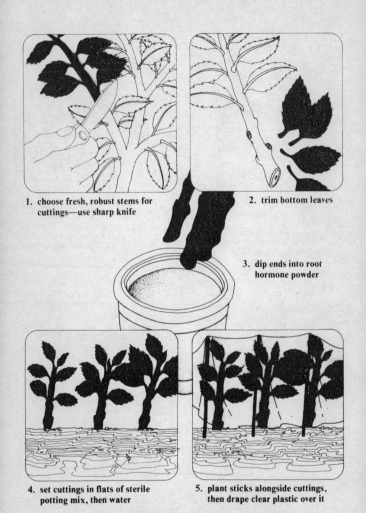

1. choose fresh, robust stems for cuttings—use sharp knife

2. trim bottom leaves

3. dip ends into root hormone powder

4. set cuttings in flats of sterile potting mix, then water

5. plant sticks alongside cuttings, then drape clear plastic over it

Starting Plants From Cuttings

16

1. separate stolon from mother plant, carefully parting roots with knife

2. separate root system, trimming dead strands

3. plant stolon, then cover with soil

4. firm soil around stolon, then water

Parting Stolons

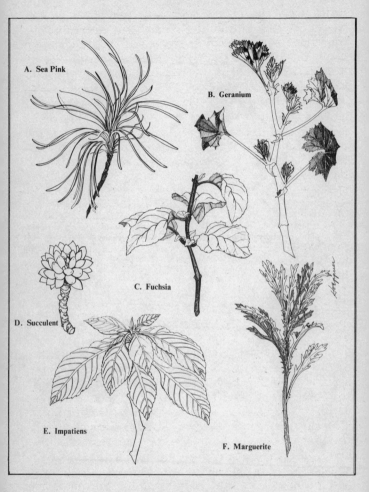

A. Sea Pink

B. Geranium

C. Fuchsia

D. Succulent

E. Impatiens

F. Marguerite

Propagation by Cuttings

varies with the plant: Some may sprout in a few weeks, others in months. Once true leaves form, transplant the seedling into pots if it is an indoor plant, or put it in the garden—weather permitting—if it is an outdoor plant. Now wait for your new plants to grow.

If you have free cuttings, the procedure is the same as far as the mechanics are concerned. The difference is that with cuttings you dip the tip of the new plant in a hormone powder to help stimulate root formation. Use shallow containers with a sterile growing medium. Cover the bed with plastic. When cuttings start to show growth they can be transplanted to serve your needs. You can also sprout new plants by using the leaves of certain species like African violets and Rex begonias; merely imbed them in growing medium. A healthy plant has hundreds of leaves; each leaf is a free new plant. Picking a few leaves does not harm the plant.

SOME HINTS

Sowing seed or starting cuttings is not really too difficult. Just do not be impatient, and if you fail, try again. Nature has bestowed many seed with "tricks" to help them survive in the wild. For example, Japanese maple seed need to be stratified for 60 to 120 days before being sown. Stratification is merely the process of keeping the seed at cool temperatures, about 40°F. You can do this by mixing the seed with sphagnum moss, putting it in a Baggie, tying the bag, and placing it in the refrigerator for the necessary time. Then remove the seed from the sphagnum and plant in shallow containers, giving routine sowing conditions. Other trees that need stratification are

9. Some seeds can be germinated in mayonaise jars in sphagnum moss. When germinated they can be removed and placed in individual pots. (PHOTO BY JACK BARNICH)

canoe birch, hackberry, eastern redbud, white ash, sweetgum, Siberian crabapple, and hemlock.

Some seed has an outer hard coating, which is a natural protective measure. Dunk these kinds of seeds in boiling water, turn off heat and leave seeds in the water for about a day. *Do not boil the seed*. After the dunking time, sow as you would ordinary seed. Hard seeds may also be aided in germinating by nicking the outer coatings with a sharp knife; this process is called scarification.

With perennials, annuals, and house plant seeds, temperature is vital to start the germination process. Generally, temperatures between 68 and 72°F. are fine for most seed. Of course, there are always exceptions, so some seed may require more coolness or heat than others.

The free pamphlets mentioned in Chapter 6 will

10. Seedling up and ready to grow in individual pot; plastic glass used to ensure humidity. (PHOTO BY JACK BARNICH)

provide you with a guide, and the Brooklyn Botanic Garden Bulletin #64 for $1.50 answers most propagation questions. Other good books on the subject include:

Plant Propagation, Principles and Practices, Hudson T. Hartman and Dale E. Kester. Englewood Cliffs, New Jersey: Prentice-Hall Inc., 1959

The Complete Book of Growing Plants from Seed, Elda Haring. New York: Hawthorn Books, Inc., 1967

Grow Your Own Plants, Jack Kramer. New York: Chas. Scribner's Sons, 1973

If you prefer to purchase seeds (none are very expensive) rather than collect your own, here are some suppliers of various kinds of plant seeds:

GENERAL SEED SUPPLIERS

W. Atlee Burpee Seed Co.
Philadelphia, Pennsylvania 19132
Clinton, Iowa 52733
Riverside, California 92502

Burgess Seed & Plant Co.
P.O. Box 1140
Galesburg, Michigan 49053

Henry Field Seed & Nursery Co.
19 N. 12th St.
Shenandoah, Iowa 51601

W. W. Olds Seed Co.
P.O. Box 1069
Madison, Wisconsin 53701

George W. Park Seed Co. Inc.
Greenwood, South Carolina 29547

Stoke's Seed Exchange
86 Exchange St.
Buffalo, New York 14205

Sutton Seeds, Ltd.
161 Bond St.
London WI, England

WILDFLOWER SEED SUPPLIERS

Clyde Robin
P.O. Box 2091
Castro Valley, California 94546

Leslie's Wildflower Nursery
30 Summer St.
Methuen, Massachusetts 01844

Nichol's Garden Nursery
1190 N. Pacific Hwy.
Albany, Oregon 97321

The list above is by no means complete; they are the companies I have done business with through the years and have found to be excellent. (For specific information on catalogs and cost see Chapter 3.)

2

WHERE TO
FIND PLANTS

If you consistently buy groceries, clothes, or plants at
one particular place, you will eventually get the best
for least, and in the bargain you might get something
for nothing too. You may buy plants at a local
nursery, a wonderful old-fashioned family operation,
a newer patio/garden shop, or in cities, at a local
florist. You may also buy at one of the department
stores or five-and-ten garden centers: Sears, Roebuck
and Company, Montgomery Ward, Woolworths, and
so on. All these plant suppliers operate in different
ways (because of necessity). Prices will vary from
place to place, so you should do comparative shop-
ping. In some cases you may find gratis plants or
giveaways, and in other places, if you know when and
how to shop, you can get plants at the lowest

11. Local nurseries have a multitude of plants in one-gallon or five-gallon cans for planting. (PHOTO BY AUTHOR)

price—almost nothing when compared to the usual selling price. Let us see what some of these plant suppliers have to offer.

LOCAL NURSERIES

The large nursery (not a wholesaler, which is something entirely different) is generally not too far from a large city and is a good place to select some but not all plants. There is an incredible assortment, and prices are generally fair, if not cheap. There are annual and perennial seedlings, a fine buy if you do not have time to start your own, and trees and shrubs, which are somewhat expensive but still satisfactory if you can afford them. Avoid buying house plants; you can buy them elsewhere at better prices. Stock in nurseries is usually very good, turnover is fast, and your chances of getting a bad plant are minimal.

If you have purchased from one nursery for some time, you may, by asking, find some plants that they are intending to discard for various reasons. Sometimes the plants are inferior, and rather than sell them, a nurseryman will simply throw them away to maintain his reputation. If you know the nursery, do not be shy; ask if you can have throwaways. It is true that many of the plants may not survive the journey home, but some will if you know how to handle them; and since this is a way to get free plants, why not give it a try? (Sometimes you may not have to ask for throwaways; a friendly supplier may give you a few plants to show good will and ensure your future business.)

Once you have the plants at home (garden or house plants), soak them in a bucket of water for several

12. Seedlings are available in flats at nurseries but will cost
more than plants you grow yourself. (PHOTO BY AUTHOR)

hours. Then put them in pots of soil with Baggies on top to ensure good humidity, and nurture them along for a few days until they show signs of new growth. When they have regained vigor, remove plastic and put them in their permanent places. Most likely, these gratis offerings will become just as healthy as newly bought plants.

At holiday time large nurseries sell seasonal plants. This is a bonanza for bargain seekers (and who isn't?). Many times whole greenhouses are cleared to make room for new plants. I once saw a truckload of Cymbidium orchids going to the dump to make room for Easter lilies. This is the time to buy, at considerable savings. Once again, some plants may live, others may not, but all you waste is your time, and with plants the odds are all in your favor. Plants have an intense urge to survive.

If your local nursery will allow you, rummage through their greenhouses. Look for the odd plant or a plant left for boarding and never picked up. The nursery owner would like the room for new plants, so make him an offer. I found a 10-foot Hylocereus for $3 and a lovely mature citrus for $5. Of course, the trick with these large plants is to get them home; if you ask for delivery, the owner may charge you three times the price of the plant, so be astute: Take your station wagon.

Most nurseries generally have sales four times a year; in spring, summer, fall, and winter. This is a good time to purchase plants for as much as 20 to 50 percent off regular prices. New stock is coming in, and old stock must be sold to make room for the new.

PATIO/GARDEN CENTERS,
DEPARTMENT STORES, FIVE-AND-TENS

The patio/garden centers may have somewhat higher prices than a large nursery because these large complexes have high rent. Stock, however, is good, but do *not* buy containers here. You can do much better by making your own containers for practically nothing or finding salvage items for still less (see Chapter 7). The patio/garden center is generally an impersonal owner/customer place, so free plants are out of the question. You may get a free boutonniere at holidays, but that is about all.

The plant departments of such large department stores as Montgomery Ward and Sears Roebuck and Company offer a large selection of all kinds of plants. They are of good quality, and turnover is fast, so chances of getting a bad plant are small. However, prices may be high except at sale times, which occur several times a year. Watch for sales in newspapers. Unfortunately, in most of these stores the garden help and advice is anything but good, so you are more or less on your own. In other words, you will have to know something about plants to get the most for your money. And once again, forget about getting any free plants.

Woolworths' and other five-and-ten stores have house and garden plant sections that have various plants at reasonable prices. These stores are good places for frugal shoppers, and even though plants may not be in tip-top shape, they are still satisfactory. Try to get to the store the day the plant shipment arrives (usually on Thursdays or Fridays, although this varies from city to city) so you can still get plants that are fresh. In such stores it is impossible for employees to water plants carefully, and in a few

13. Local florists have a fine array of plants and gift items.
(PHOTO BY JAMES CAREW)

days time, good plants may become bad ones.
Enough said! Get there early.

LOCAL FLORISTS

Local florist shops are beautiful places, and I
admire them. They have lovely flowers and absolutely
top plants, but prices are tops too! Buy from florists
if you must, but theirs is a specialty business: The
plants sold are usually more for accommodation than
anything else. Most florists make their big dollar on
cut flowers and funeral and wedding arrangements.
At seasonal times, however, florists sell poinsettias for
Christmas, Easter lilies for Easter, Azaleas for
Mothers' Day, and so on. If you have time, visit your
local florist the day after the holiday. Invariably there
will still be some gift plants around, and generally
they will be priced very reasonably; for example,
azaleas that were $10 the day before may now be
selling for $2.

HOUSE PLANT STORES, BOUTIQUES

In between the fine florist shop and the old-
fashioned nursery there is a new category: the house
plant stores and boutiques. The merchandise includes
containers, terrariums, and oddments, as well as
plants. The stores I have scouted have turned out to
be excellent places to buy inexpensive house plants,
and sometimes they stock hard-to-find plants. The
owners of these places are generally more interested
in plants than the large concern (whose buyer may
have several departments to care for). As a result, the
owner knows his plants by name and knows how to

14. This charming plant boutique specializes in house plants. Many such establishments are appearing throughout the country where service is good and information valid. (PHOTO BY MATTHEW BARR)

care for them. What is more fortunate is that these growing concerns sell plants at reasonable prices. The markup is rarely over 25 percent, so you can get a lot for your money. Also, if there is only one plant of a kind, and you express interest in it, do not be surprised to get a cutting for free (this is not common practice, but it does happen)! Let us hope that these new types of plant stores make the grade because we need the personal touch and the fair exchange.

OTHER PLACES

Flea markets are springing up in many areas. These places usually specialize in furniture, but recently I have found and bought excellent plants for practically nothing: large cacti for $2 and $3, Philodendrons for $1, and a rare contorted ivy species for $2—a species that I could never find if I hunted nurseries for years. Do not be finicky about how the plant looks. Even if the mature plant is dead, there will be some offsprings—stolons or offshoots—that can be salvaged, and even if you pay $1, you are far ahead of the game.

Garage sales promise to be good hunting grounds for inexpensive plants, but they generally turn out to be less than desirable simply because people are moving, and their plants, like their pets, are valuable and so are the prices. It is better to look elsewhere.

Moving companies occasionally have unclaimed furniture—and plant—sales. This is where you can find excellent bargains in plants. Unfortunately, these bonanzas are infrequent, but watch newspaper classified ads, where you occasionally will see notice of such sales.

15. Another indoor plant store where all kinds of house plants from miniatures for terrariums to decorator plants can be purchased at reasonable cost. (PHOTO BY JAMES CAREW)

SALE PLANTS YOU SEE

Words to the wise from most sources are "Never, never buy anything on sale." Fie on such words. There is nothing wrong with a sale plant as long as the price is right and you know how to take care of it once you get it home. Just remember that with sale plants you have to get there early and pick the best of the bunch.

Sales at local nurseries are fine, but better yet are sales at public arboretums or conservatories. Generally, these places have a once-a-year sale to make space; you can find rare plants for next-to-nothing prices. The key to success is to know what kind of plant you are buying. None, of course, will cost too much, but remember that you want your money's worth. Look for fresh healthy plants. Sales at arboretums are busy and crowded because very good plants are offered. These sales are not to be confused with sales at retail nurseries, where more common plants of perhaps lesser quality are offered.

SALE PLANTS YOU DO NOT SEE

Sale plants or free ones from mail-order houses usually are offered in a "buy six, get one for free policy." There is nothing wrong with this kind of buying; just learn to take advantage of it. In many cases the one-for-free offer (discounts too) is somewhere in the catalog, but you might miss it, so read order blanks carefully. Because most mail-order sources are reputable people and want your business, they are not going to try to mislead you. You may be buying sight-unseen, but usually you will get good plants.

Frequently, specific plants such as palms or lilies are offered in large-page advertisements of various magazines. Buyer beware! Generally these are small plants, and buying from a picture can fool you because the picture always looks better than the plant you get: the photograph shows a 5-foot palm for $2; what you usually receive is a 2-inch plant that *eventually* might grow to 5 feet. But, like people climbing Mt. Everest, only a few make it.

CLASSIFIED ADS

Classified plant ads are generally at the end of the garden magazines or newspapers and are fine sources for specialty plants. The classifieds are nominally priced for the advertiser, and you invariably get good plants. I order from these ads frequently, with excellent results.

To be specifically clear about garden ads in garden magazines, let me say again that most of the plants offered are satisfactory, and you will get your money's worth. What I am trying to warn you against are glamorous ads in living color for plants that just may not live up to their enthusiastic copy. So when you read ads for plants beware of exaggerated claims. And avoid ads that specify exotic names and descriptions for whatever plants they sell. Remember that ads (especially in color) in magazines cost a great deal, and someone has to pay for them; it could be you.

3

CATALOGS AND OTHER PUBLICATIONS

Mail-order plant suppliers throughout the country provide a wealth of plants and some sound garden information in their catalogs. Some of the catalogs are indeed breathtaking, with vivid color pictures, good advice, and textural information about an incredible array of plants (botanical names and their cultivation, for example).

Some mail-order suppliers specialize in orchids, others in annuals and perennials, some in indoor plants, and even a few in rhododendrons or iris. There is something for everyone. Remember that a specialist in one particular plant family is more apt to know his plants as individual things of beauty rather than commodities to sell. His interest is to your benefit when buying.

For years I have bought plants from various mail-order companies throughout the United States, and always, with rare exception, I have been well pleased. But before you buy anything write for catalogs; many are free or cost hardly more than $1. It will be the wisest money you will invest.

MAIL-ORDER CATALOGS

Some mail-order companies' catalogs can make a gardener out of a nongardener. The color photographs are incredibly beautiful, but do not ever think you can achieve these all-season, all-colorful gardens without spending a bundle. Be practical. It takes years to achieve that garden of your dreams, but do study the pictures and names because from these catalogs you can easily learn plant names and identification. In particular, when you get these mail-order catalogs learn the terms annual and perennial, deciduous trees and shrubs, needle evergreen and broad-leaf evergreens. This information will be a great help to you when you put a garden together.

In addition to the pictures, some companies such as Park's, Wayside, and White Flower Farm offer a wealth of information about plants and planting in their publications. Many times you do almost as well paying the $1 or $2 for the catalog as you do paying $10 for a hardcover book about gardening (may book publishers forgive me). But these are the exceptions. Most companies have simple catalogs and listings that leave a great deal to be desired. Yet, they are usually free, and if nothing else you will learn the proper botanical names of plants.

Some companies offer a variety of garden plants,

but others, as mentioned, may be specialists in such plants as roses, iris, or lilies. Some concentrate on house plants, and places such as Merry Gardens offer excellent plants at fair prices; for example, a 3-inch seedling may cost only $1. If you have a favorite plant family—begonias or African violets—these specialized companies are the ones to buy from. You get up-to-the-minute hybrids and a choice you would never find in any store. Another advantage of mail-order plants is that if you order about ten plants, you generally get a few free. This may not be stated in the catalog and may not be true in all places, but usually there are small bonuses included from some sources. Once again, know what you are buying. Write for catalogs first, look them over carefully, and then make selections by plant name (not common name) so you get what you want.

As mentioned, most mail-order plant suppliers are reputable and you get your money's worth. However, as with all businesses, there are some suppliers that do not deliver what they promise. Recently, the Better Business Bureau has been scrutinizing mail-order houses that supply shade trees. To quote from a recent newspaper article in the *San Francisco Chronicle*, dated May 31, 1973: "Over the years a few mail order promotion firms have been found to exploit certain plants, making false claims as to their growth and performance. Typically they select one plant or tree each season and really push it through direct mail advertising, radio and newspaper ads. Usually the item offered is likely to be nothing more than a very common plant or weed."

The BBB suggests (and I agree with them) that prospective purchasers check out the firms's claims by comparing its catalog with those of other companies offering plants of the same kind, size, and quality.

For a copy of "Consumer Tips on Mail Order Shade Trees," send a self-addressed, stamped envelope to the Better Business Bureau of your city.

MAIL-ORDER SUPPLIERS

The following list of suppliers are those which I have dealt with through the years and those which friends have recommended. Their listing here does not, however, necessarily constitute an endorsement of their plants. (This is not a complete list but rather those companies I know about.)

TREES, SHRUBS, ANNUALS, PERENNIALS

Burgess Seed & Plant Co.
P.O. Box 218
Galesburg, Michigan 49053

Shrubs and trees, perennials, vegetables. Approx. 80-page *Garden Guide*, free.

Burnett Brothers, Inc.
92 Chambers St.
New York, New York 10007

All kinds of plants. 52-page color catalog, free.

W. Atlee Burpee Co.
Hunting Park at 18th
Philadelphia,
Pennsylvania 19132

Shrubs, trees, perennials, annuals, vegetables. Extensive 165-page color catalog, free.

Earl Ferris Nursery
376 Bridge St.
Hampton, Iowa 50441

All kinds of plants. 48-page color catalog, free.

Henry Field Seed & Nursery Co. Shenandoah, Iowa 51601	Shrubs and trees, perennials, vegetables. 128-page color catalog, free.
Inter-State Nurseries 523 E St. Hamburg, Iowa 51640	Shrubs and trees, perennials, vegetables. 8-page catalog, free.
Kelly Bros. Nursery 23 Maple St. Danville, New York 14437	Shrubs and trees, vines, bulbs, fruit trees. 400-page color catalog, free.
Krider Nurseries, Inc. P.O. Box 193 Midolobury, Indiana 46540	Trees, roses, evergreens, perennials, annuals. Colorful 40-page catalog, free.
Earl May Seed Co. 3127 Elm St. Shenandoah, Iowa 51601	Shrubs and trees, fruit trees, vines, roses. Color landscaping/garden catalog, free.
Musser Forests Indiana, Pennsylvania 15701	Trees, flowers, vegetables, other plants. Color catalog, free.
Old Seed Co. P.O. Box 1069, Dept. G Madison, Wisconsin 53701	All kinds of plants. 84-page color catalog, free.
George W. Park Seed Co. Greenwood, South Carolina 29646	Shrubs and trees, perennials, annuals. Extensive 115-page indexed color catalog, free.

Robeson Quality Seeds, Inc.
Hall, New York 14463

Vegetables, flowers.
Catalog, free.

R. H. Shumway Seedsman
Rockford, Illinois 61101

Plant and nursery
catalog, free.

Stark Brothers
P.O. Box A 24773
Louisiana, Missouri 63353

Roses, fruit trees,
other plants. 35-page
garden and landscape
catalog, free.

Stern Nurseries
Geneva, New York 14456

Shrubs and trees,
perennials, other
plants. 67-page
catalog, 50 cents.

Stokes Seeds, Inc.
P.O. Box 548
Buffalo, New York 14240

Vegetables, flowers,
other plants. Good
catalog, free.

Wayside Gardens
Mentor, Ohio 44060

Shrubs and trees,
perennials, annuals.
Extensive 97-page
color catalog, $1.

White Flower Farm
Litchfield, Connecticut
06759

Perennials, annuals,
other plants. Definitive
100-page catalog, $2.

BULBS, CORMS, TUBERS

Antonelli Brothers
2545 Capitola Rd.
Santa Cruz, California
95060

Begonias, achimenes,
dahlias. 26-page color
brochure, free.

P. De Jager & Sons, Inc.
188 Ashbury St.
S. Hamilton, Massachusetts
01982

Bulbs of all kinds. 25-page color catalog with planting instruction, free.

International Growers
Exchange Inc.
P.O. Box 397
Farmington, Michigan
48024

Wide World of Bulbs and Plants: catalog, $2.

Michigan Bulb Co.
Grand Rapids, Michigan
49506

Shrubs, trees, flowers, evergreens, fruits. Garden catalog, free.

George W. Park Seed Co.
Greenwood, South Carolina
29646

Bulb catalog at seasonal times, free.

John Scheepers, Inc.
63 Wall St.
New York, New York 10005

Bulbs, corms, tubers. 56-page color catalog with planting tips, free.

Van Bourgondien Bros.
245 Farmingdale Rd.
Rt. 109
Babylon, New York 11702

Bulbs, corms, tubers. 15-page color catalog, free.

Wayside Gardens
Mentor, Ohio 44060

Bulb catalog at seasonal times, free.

ROSES

Armstrong Roses
P.O. Box 473
Ontario, California 91761

Many kinds of roses. Catalog, free.

Jackson & Perkins Co.
Rose Lane
Medford, Oregon 97501

Glamorous color catalog mainly limited to roses and lilies, free.

Star Roses & Star Mums
The Conard-Pyle Co.
West Grove, Pennsylvania 19390

Does not ship into California. Catalog limited to mums and roses, free.

Thomasville Nurseries, Inc.
P.O. Box 7
Thomasville, Georgia 31792

Mainly roses. 24-page catalog, free.

Tillotson's Roses
Brown's Valley Rd.
Watsonville, California 95076

Roses. Exquisitely done, 78-page indexed booklet, $1.

Wyant Roses
Rt. 84, Johnny Cake Ridge
Mentor, Ohio 44060

Old roses, new roses. Catalog, free.

IRIS

Bay View Gardens
1201 Bay St.
Santa Cruz, California 95060

Good selection of all kinds of iris; 14-page booklet with some pictures, free.

Cooley's Gardens
Silverton, Oregon 97381

Large iris selection. 55-page color catalog, free.

Melrose Gardens
309 Best Rd. South
Stockton, California 95206

Fine selection of iris. 26-page catalog, free.

Riverdale Iris Gardens
7124 Riverdale Rd.
Minneapolis, Minnesota
55430

Good selection of iris.
42-page catalog, free.

Schreiner's Gardens, Inc.
3625 Quimaby Rd. N.E.
Salem, Oregon 97303

Outstanding iris
selection. 72-page
color catalog, free.

Gilbert Wild & Son, Inc.
Sarcoxie, Missouri 64862

Peony, iris, daylily.
92-page color catalog
listing 1300 varieties
of plants, 50 cents.

DWARF CONIFERS

Girard Nurseries
Geneva, Ohio 44041

Catalog, free.

Mayfair Nurseries
Rt. 2, P.O. Box 68
Nichols, New York 13812

Dwarf conifers,
heathers, dwarf shrubs.
44-page catalog, 25
cents.

ALPINE AND ROCK GARDEN PLANTS

Carroll Gardens
P.O. Box 310
Westminster, Maryland
21157

Perennials and rock
plants. Excellent 69-
page catalog, free.

Lamb Nurseries
E. 101 Sharp Ave.
Spokane, Washington
99202

Hardy perennials and
rock plants. 52-page
catalog, free.

Siskiyou Rare Plant Nursery
522 Franquette St.
Medford, Oregon 97501

All kinds of alpines
and ferns. 24-page
catalog, 50 cents.

RHODODENDRONS

Warren Baldsoefen
P.O. Box 88
Bellvale, New York 10912

Rhododendrons and
azaleas. 66-page color
catalog, $1.

Carlson's Gardens
P.O. Box 305
South Salem, New York
10590

Azaleas and
rhododendrons. 12-
page listing, free.

Greer Gardens
1280 Goodpasture Island
Rd.
Eugene, Oregon 97401

Mainly rhododendrons
and azaleas. 20-page
brochure, free.

DAHLIAS

E. Ray Miller's Dahlia
Gardens
167 N.E. 12th Ave.
Hillsboro, Oregon 97123

Dahlias of all kinds.
15-page brochure, free.

S & K Gardens
401 Quick Rd.
Castle Rock, Washington
98611

All kinds of dahlias.
32-page catalog, free.

Swan Island Dahlias
P.O. Box 800
Canby, Oregon 97013

All kinds of mums.
40-page fine color
catalog, 75 cents.

CHRYSANTHEMUMS

Dooley Gardens
Rt. 1
Hutchinson, Minnesota
55350

Fair selection of
mums. 12-page
booklet (no pictures),
free.

Sunnyslope Gardens
8638 Huntington Dr.
San Gabriel, California
91788

All kinds of mums.
30-page catalog (some
color), free.

DAYLILIES

Howell Gardens
1587 Letitia St.
Baton Rouge, Louisiana
70808

Good selection of
daylilies. Catalog, free.

Hughes Gardens
Hwy. 287
Rt. 1, P.O. Box 127-C
Mansfield, Texas 76063

Large selection of
daylilies. 13-page
catalog, free.

Mission Gardens
Techny, Illinois 60082

Daylilies and peonies.
20-page booklet, free.

Gilbert Wild & Son, Inc.
Sarcoxie, Missouri 64862

Daylilies. Large
catalog (See Iris
listing), free.

HERBS

Hilltop Herb Farm
P.O. Box 866
Cleveland, Texas 77327

Herbs of all kinds. 4-
page printed brochure,
35 cents.

Mincemoyer's Nursery
County Line Rd., Rt. 526
Jackson, New Jersey 08527

Herbs of all kinds. 16-
page booklet (no
pictures), 25 cents.

Nichols Garden Nursery
1190 Pacific Hwy.
Albany, Oregon 97321

Large selection of
herbs and other plants.
30-page catalog, 25
cents.

Putney Nursery, Inc.
Putney, Vermont 05346

(See Wild flowers
listing)

Sunnybrook Farms Nursery
9448 Mayfield Rd.
Chesterland, Ohio 44026

Herbs, geraniums, and
other plants. 36-page
booklet, 50 cents.

EPIPHYLLUMS

Beahm Gardens
2686 Paloma St.
Pasadena, California 91107

Epiphyllum and
related species. 33-
page black and white
catalog, free.

Hawk's Epiphyllum Nursery
Dept. H., 11918 E. Lambert
El Monte, California 91732

Good catalog of
epiphyllum species
with price list, 35
cents.

WILDFLOWERS

Ferndale Nursery
P.O. Box 218
Askov, Minnesota 55704

Hardy wildflowers and
ferns. Lists, free (send
stamped, self-
addressed envelope).

Griffey's Nursery
Rt. 3, P.O. Box 17A
Marshall, North Carolina
28753

Native wildflowers,
shrubs, vines, ever-
greens. Catalog, free.

Leslie's Wildflower Nursery
30 Summer St.
Hethuen, Massachusetts
01844

12-page catalog,
25 cents.

Lounsberry Gardens
P.O. Box 135
Oakford, Illinois 62673

Good selection of
wildflowers. Catalog,
25 cents.

Midwest Wildflowers
P.O. Box 64B
Rockton, Illinois 61072

Seed; fact, folklore
and culture.
Wildflower catalog,
25 cents.

Mincemoyer's Nursery
County Line Rd., Rt. 526
Jackson, New Jersey 08527

(See Herb listing.)

Putney Nurseries, Inc.
Putney, Vermont 05346

Many wildflowers. 32-
page catalog (many
photos), 25 cents.

Clyde Robin
P.O. Box 2091
Castro Valley, California
94546

Many different wild
plants. 103-page color
catalog, $1.

INDOOR PLANTS

Alberts & Merkel Bros.
2210 S. Federal Hwy.
Boynton Beach, Florida
33435

House plants of all
kinds. 68-page color
catalog, 50 cents.

Arthur Eames Allgrove
North Wilmington,
Massachusetts 01877

Terrarium plants,
bonsai and saekei
plants. Newspaper-
type fine catalog, 50
cents.

Fischer Greenhouses
Linwood, New Jersey
08221

African violets and
other gesneriads. 20-
page color catalog, 60
cents.

House Plant Corner
P.O. Box 165-P
Oxford, Maryland 21654

House plants and
supplies. Illustrated
catalog, 25 cents.

Kartuz Greenhouses
92H Chestnut St.
Wilmington,
Massachusetts 01887

Begonias, gesneriads,
geraniums. Good
illustrated catalog,
50 cents.

Logee's Greenhouses
55 North St.
Danielson, Connecticut
06239

House plants,
begonias, geraniums.
Extensive 72-page
color catalog, 25 cents
(and well worth it).

Lyndon Lyons
14 Mutchler St.
Dolgeville, New York
13329

African violets and
other gesneriads. Fold-
out listing, free.

McComb's Greenhouses
New Straitsville, Ohio
43766

Terrarium plants,
ferns. Illustrated
catalog, 35 cents.

Merry Gardens
Camden, Maine 04843

House plants of all
kinds; extensive
selection. 15-page
catalog, 25 cents.

Julius Roehrs
Rt. 33
Farmingdale, New Jersey
07727

Good selection of indoor plants; large sizes also available. Catalog, free.

Tinari Greenhouses
2325 Valley Rd.,
P.O. Box 190
Huntingdon Valley,
Pennsylvania 19006

Indoor plants of many kinds. 16-page color brochure, free.

CACTI AND SUCCULENTS

Cactus Gem Nursery
Dept. H., P.O. Box 327
Aromas, California 95004

5000 different species. Price list, free.

Cactus by Mueller
10411 Rosedale Hwy.
Bakersfield, California
93308

Good selection of cacti. Price list, 8 cents.

Davis Cactus Gardens
1522 Jefferson St.
Kerrville, Texas 78028

Many cacti and succulents. Catalog, 25 cents.

Desert Plant Co.
P.O. Box 880
Marfa, Texas 79843

Illustrated cactus catalog, 50 cents.

Henrietta's Cactus Nursery
1345 N. Brawley
Fresno, California 93705

Very large selection of cacti. Extensive fine catalog, 20 cents.

ORCHIDS

Hausermann Orchids
P.O. 363
Elmhurst, Illinois 60218

Excellent selection of species orchids. 40-page color catalog, free.

Margaret Ilgenfritz Orchids
P.O. Box 665
Monroe, Michigan 48161

Listing of many orchids. Fine catalog, $1.

Jones & Scully Inc.
2200 N.W. 33rd Ave.
Miami, Florida 33142

All kinds of orchids. 140-page superlative color catalog. $2 (and worth it).

GREENHOUSES

Aluminum Greenhouses, Inc.
14615 Lorain Ave.
Cleveland, Ohio 44111

Home Greenhouses: a 28-page brochure on prefabricated aluminum greenhouses; plans included, 25 cents.

Lord & Burnham
Irvington, New York 10533

Window Greenhouses; Home Greenhouses: a booklet on all types of greenhouses, free.

Sudbury Laboratory Inc.
P.O. Box 1218
Sudbury, Massachusetts
01776

Acid Alkali Preference lists: an invaluable folder with optimum pH ranges for 300 different plants, free.

Sudbury Laboratory Inc.
P.O. Box 1218
Sudbury, Massachusetts
01776

The Good Earth: a 24-page brochure on soil testing, with comments on nitrogen, phosphorus, and potash; a necessary booklet for the organic gardener, 25 cents.

WATER GARDENS

Slocum Water Gardens
1101 Cypress Garden Rd.
Winterhaven, Florida 33880

Everything for the Lily Pool: a booklet covering water gardening and gardens, 25 cents.

Three Springs Fisheries, Inc.
4613 Main Rd.
Lilyponds, Maryland 21717

What You Should Know about Water Lilies: a color catalog of many water lilies; hints and suggestions about building pools, 50 cents.

Van Ness Water Gardens
Rt. 1
Upland, California 91786

Water Lilies: a superior colorful catalog with pool supplies and information, 10 cents.

William Tricker, Inc.
Saddle River, New Jersey
07458
          or
Independence, Ohio 44131

Tricker's Water Lilies: a handsomely illustrated 32-page catalog on all kinds of water plants and pumps, free.

FOUNTAINS

Rain Jet Corp.
301 S. Flower St.
Dept. FBR
Burbank, California 91503

Fountains: a lovely catalog on fountain assemblies for landscaping, free.

LANDSCAPING BOOKLETS

Featherock, Inc.
6331 Hollywood Blvd.
Los Angeles, California
90028

Stone Landscaping: a 22-page book of hints and ideas on using featherock stone, free.

Stark Brothers
Louisiana, Missouri 63353

How to Plan Landscape Planting: a 16-page color booklet of planting and selection information, free.

Wayside Gardens
Mentor, Ohio 44060

Wayside Gardens Planting and Cultural Guide: a 32-page booklet on the planting of all kinds of plants, with hints and suggestions, $1.

Wayside Gardens
Mentor, Ohio 44060

Cultural Information on Perennial Plants: a 48-page booklet on when and how to plant, featuring over 220 different perennials, $2

Davey Trees
Kent, Ohio 44240

Guide to Tree Beauty and Care: a 36-page booklet on pruning, fertilizing, cabeling, bracing, $1.

MULCHES

Hershey Estates
Dept. Q
Hershey, Pennsylvania

All about Mulching: a good pamphlet on using mulches on plants and shrubs, free.

SHIPPING PLANTS

What is the best method of transportation to get plants from suppliers to your home? You can leave this to the supplier, but generally delivery will not be the fastest way.

There are many ways to ship plants; it is worthwhile to investigate them all if you want fast service. There are also many different prices, so it is wise to check things out carefully.

If there is no great rush, plants can be shipped parcel post; this is the most reasonable way. Special Handling for parcel post costs a little more but is worth it because it expedites the shipment. Air mail is expensive but does bring the plants to you overnight, or the second day at the latest. Check with your local post office about box-size limitations because 100 inches is maximum (length plus girth combined) for packages.

An excellent way of receiving plants is Air Freight Collect, if you are ordering many plants. Rates are based on 100 pounds, so whether you ship 10 or 100 pounds the price is the same. For example, from Illinois to California the rate is about $19 per 100 pounds, and delivery is overnight. There will be an extra charge for truck service from airport to your home; generally I pick up my own plants to save the fee. On air freight shipments have the supplier include your phone number on the outside of the package so you can be called when plants arrive.

Railway Express shipping is still another way to go. Service is good for short distances, but quite costly for long distances. Also, as with the post office, there are box-size limitations, so check before shipping plants.

A reasonably priced shipping service is Greyhound or Continental Bus Lines, if they operate within your area. This takes longer than other means of shipping and you must pick up plants at the nearest station, but it is cheaper than Air Freight or Railway Express.

United Parcel Service (UPS) is another way to ship plants, but there are restrictions, so check with your local office. Box size is limited to 108 inches (length plus girth combined), but rates are relatively moderate and service excellent. Within the state of California service is fine, with delivery overnight or on the second day to most points. However, they are not able to ship by air to Illinois or New York because they are not licensed for this service, according to information given me.

Don't fret about the packing of plants; suppliers generally pack plants with care, sufficiently protected from heat and cold. If, however, plants do arrive in bad shape, notify the supplier at once. Do not wait; it you do, your claim may not be honored.

MANUFACTURERS' CATALOGS

America has a vast complex of manufacturing companies producing many diversified products. As in all fields, the manufacturers of garden products offer everything from herbicides to fertilizers, containers to pruning shears, and mowers to mulches, in an incredible assemblage of lotions, potions, machines, and tools—you name it. Some are small companies, others are large, and several offer free gardening brochures (sometimes available at nurseries or sent by mail to you). For the most part, these are lovely colorful publications with sound information. However, remember while reading these publications that you will not get something for nothing. The brochures have a definite purpose—*to sell you their product*—be it an insecticide, pruning shears, lawn mower or what have you. Be wary, and read closely and carefully before you buy what you may not ever need to keep a garden growing. Remember that years ago, long before gardening aids, there were lovely gardens. Think about it. My grandmother has a fine garden and never used any manufactured products to tend or defend it. Work was what made the garden grow, and even though modern conveniences and aids are nice, and may do the job they say they do, they very often are not needed in the average garden.

Do not confuse manufacturers' publications with free catalogs issued by various industry associations such as the California Redwood Association, Western Wood Products, or Bulb Growers Association. There is a difference; the industry association publications offer ideas for the consumer on how to use a product the best way or how best to grow a certain plant. In other words, a specified manufactured item is not being sold as such. You have a choice of buying lumber or tile or cement from different dealers; you can buy roses or bulbs from hundreds of different nurseries.

By all means, write for the excellent publications from association industries. Some have elaborate plans and details on how-to-do-it projects. Some of the brochures are so complete you may not have to refer to any other source. Generally, there is a minimum charge for the publications. Here are four association services that have supplied me with excellent printed matter on a variety of things:

California Redwood Assoc.
617 Montgomery St.
San Francisco, California
94111

Brochures: Redwood Fences; Redwood Decks; Redwood Garden Fences. Plans available.

Western Wood Products Assoc.
Yeon Bldg.
Portland, Oregon 97204

Brochures: New Ideas on Outdoor Living; Patios, Fences.

American Plywood Assoc.
119 A St.
Tacoma, Washington 98401

Brochures: Modular Plant Boxes; Portable Planters; Screens; Potting Benches.

Netherlands Flower Bulb Inst.
29 Broadway
New York, New York 10006

Beautiful color brochure on all kinds of bulbs. Planting guide.

Large conglomerates have recently stepped into the gardening field (diversification, it is called); they offer roses, lilies, and other plants. These companies have a nationwide advertising campaign of monumental dimensions. However, what is advertised may be no better and in some cases, may be inferior to the offerings of the average rose or lily grower (who can not afford such costly ads). Remember that someone must pay for advertising; in most cases it is you! Accept the free brochures, but do not feel obligated to buy. They solicited you; you did not go to them.

A number of companies also advertise something for nothing—a small plant, a package of seed—and again there is a reason. True, the promised gift is free and costs nothing more than the time to fill out the offer blank. But by applying for the free gift from that supplier you may find your name on what is known as a garden mailing list. These lists are compiled and then sold by various sources to companies for direct mail advertising. So if you often wondered how Joe Moe Bulb Company got your name when their literature appears in your mail box, now you know. You have exchanged your name and your privacy for a 10-cent plant! Be wary.

GARDEN BOOKS

I have written over thirty gardening books, and so to indulge in this section is like putting my head in a guillotine. Still, because there are so many garden books—paper and hardcover—I feel obligated to share my knowledge about them.

There are gift and how-to-do-it books, books on specific plants, and technical books on gardening. Some books are filled with glorious color photographs that stimulate even the non-gardener; these are high-priced volumes generally purchased as gifts. They are fun to look at, but many lack solid garden information. Also in this category are some important books (usually from England or Holland) that are distributed by publishers here. These books make fine reading for English gardeners, but plant names and gardening procedures are somewhat different in our country.

Technical books are also available for the advanced gardener, but for most people, they are simply too verbose, and are apt to confuse rather than help home gardeners. However, a basic book on botany or plant nomenclature is sometimes a good buy.

There are many hardcover books, but paperbacks are increasing. There are originals and reprints of old works or of new best-selling books. Some paperbacks are reprints of hardback books with new covers, which is difficult to know unless you read the fine print on the front page. There is nothing wrong with a paperback book of a good recent hardcover book, or for that matter, of a very old one, but when you have purchased a hardcover for $7 a few years before and then buy it at $3 just for the new cover, you are bound to get angry. (I know I was.) So before you buy a paperback be sure you have not already bought it before in hardcover form.

There are also hardcover books that are collections of various articles from a specific magazine. I suppose there is nothing wrong with this, but after I bought one such book, all information—and photos—looked familiar. As I read further I recalled reading most of the material in past issues of the magazine through the years. Thus, I paid good money for material I already had digested at one time or another. Magazines also offer a compilation in once-a-year softcovers (generally in spring). They publish the best articles from previous years' issues in one lavish publication. This is feasible for those people who do not subscribe to the magazine regularly, and is perhaps a bargain. However, if you regularly subscribe to the magazine, you will be annoyed to realize you already had seen most of the information before in past issues.

Just how many gardening books do you need to get a start in gardening? Actually, five or six good books can give you a fairly comprehensive picture of gardening. The list that follows are some of the books I always have on hand:

GENERAL GARDEN BOOKS

McCall's Garden Book, Gretchen Fischer Harshbarger. New York: Simon and Schuster, 1967

The Complete Illustrated Book of Garden Magic, revised and edited by Marjorie Dietz. New York: Doubleday, 1971

Helen Van Pelt Wilson's Own Garden and Landscape Book, Helen Van Pelt Wilson. New York: Doubleday, 1973

Better Homes & Gardens, New Garden Book, Des Moines, Meredith 1971

TREES AND SHRUBS

Trees for American Gardens, Donald Wyman, New York: Macmillan, 1968

Shrubs and Vines for American Gardens, Donald Wyman. New York: Macmillan, 1969

The Tree Identification Book, George W. D. Symonds, New York: William Morrow, 1958 (now also in paperback)

INDOOR GARDEN BOOKS

1000 Beautiful House Plants and How to Grow Them, Jack Kramer. William Morrow, 1969 (paperback version, 1973)

Garden In Your House, revised edition, Ernesta Drinker Ballard. New York: Harper & Row, 1972

World Book of House Plants, Elvin McDonald. New York: World Publishing, 1963 (paperback version, 1970)

New York Times Book of House Plants, Joan Faust. New York: Quadrangle Books, 1973

BASIC BOTANY BOOKS

Botany Made Simple, Victor A. Greutach. New York: Doubleday, 1968

The World of Plant Life, Clarance J. Hylander. New York: Macmillan, 1956

ORGANIC GARDENING

Gardening Without Poisons, Beatrice Trum Hunter. Boston: Houghton, Mifflin, 1964 (now also in paperback)

Organic Gardening Without Poison, Hamilton Tyler. New York: Van Nostrand Reinhold, 1970

The Natural Way to Pest Free Gardening, Jack Kramer. New York: Scribner's, 1972

The above books (one from each category) should give you a start in gardening. With your books and the basic gardening pamphlets from the United States Government Printing Office (at little cost) you should be well on your way with spade in hand and knowledge in your head. (See Chapter 6 for Government publications.) The publications from the Brooklyn Botanic Gardens are also excellent (and reasonably priced). (See Chapter 6.)

Now, seek books about specific subjects you may be interested in—water gardening, fruit trees, philodendrons, terrarium gardening, and so forth.

Just how do you tell a good book from a bad one? Look for solid information and not generalities or rehashed material; study photographs to be sure they relate to the text, and are not just added for beauty. Look for how-to drawings that make gardening easy. Avoid books that have numerous photos supplied by national manufacturers; the products may be fine, but many times free photos to authors do not relate to the copy.

CHAPTER
4

4

PLANT SOCIETIES AND FLOWER SHOWS

NATIONAL PLANT SOCIETIES

When you first start gardening you may think it unnecessary to join plant societies or know about them. Yet societies that specialize in specific plants— begonias, camellias, ferns, and so forth—offer many advantages to the gardener, including information not otherwise available. The publications of national plant societies contain know-how from growers all over the country and answer your questions about plants. Occasionally you will also find seed for free, and other times for a slight charge (25 or 50 cents) in the journals. These will be seed of hard-to-get plants that you could never buy at nurseries. Other advantages of the journals include photographs for identification and a potpourri of good information on your favorite plant. I am a member of five different national plant societies—orchids, bromeliads, begonias, ferns, indoor light gardening—and I keep their publications from year to year. If ever I am in doubt about specific growing methods, I check the bulletins and invariably find my answer. All this for a nominal yearly fee. These plant societies serve a definite purpose and are a working tool for the average public, all for a very nominal membership fee: average yearly dues are $5. Following is a list of national plant societies; write for membership fees and information:

LIST OF PLANT SOCIETIES

African Violet Society of America, Inc.
P.O. Box 1326
Knoxville, Tennessee 37901

African Violet Magazine
5 times per year.

American Begonia Society, Inc.
1431 Coronado Terr.
Los Angeles, California 90026

The Begonian
Monthly

The American Bonsai Society
Herbert R. Brauner, Membership Sec.
229 North Shore Dr.
Lake Waukomis
Parksville, Missouri 64151

Bonsai Quarterly

The American Boxwood Society
P.O. Box 85
Boyce, Virginia 22620

The Boxwood Bulletin
Quarterly

The American Camellia
Society
P.O. Box 212
Fort Valley, Georgia 31030

The Camellia Journal

The American Daffodil
Society, Inc.
89 Chichester Rd.
New Canaan, Connecticut
06840

The Daffodil Journal
Quarterly

The American Dahlia
Society, Inc.
Mrs. Caroline Meyer
92-21 W. Delaware Dr.
Mystic Islands
Tuckerton, New Jersey
07087

*Bulletin of the
American Dahlia
Society*
Quarterly

American Fern Society
Dept. of Botany
Univ. of Tennessee
Knoxville, Tennessee 37916

American Fern Journal
Quarterly

The American Fuchsia
Society
Mrs. Lillian Lee, Sec.
738 22nd Ave.
San Francisco, California
94121

*American Fuchsia
Society Bulletin*
Monthly

The American Gesneriad
Society
Mr. Edgar Sherer
11983 Darlington Ave.
Los Angeles, California
90049

*Gesneriad Saintpaulia
News* Bimonthly

The American Gloxinia
and Gesneriad Society, Inc.
Mrs. Diantha Buell, Sec.
Dept. AHS
Eastford, Connecticut
06242

The Gloxinian
Bimonthly

American Gourd Society
John Stevens, Treas.
RR 1, P.O. Box 274
Mt. Gilead, Ohio 43338

The Gourd 3 times per
year

American Hemerocallis
Society
Mrs. Lewis B. Wheeler, Sec.
P.O. Box 586
Woodstock, Illinois 60098

*The Hemerocallis
Journal* Quarterly

The American Hibiscus
Society
P.O. Box 98
Eagle Lake, Florida 33839

Seed Pod Quarterly

The American Hosta
Society
Mrs. Glen Fisher
4392 W. 20th Street Rd.
Oshkosh, Wisconsin 54901

*The American Hosta
Society Newsletter
Bulletin of the
American Hosta
Society*

The American Iris Society
Clifford W. Benson, Exec.
Sec.
2315 Tower Grove Ave.
St. Louis, Missouri 63110

*Bulletin of the
American Iris Society*
Quarterly

The American Magnolia Society
Philip J. Savage, Jr., Sec.-Treas.
2150 Woodward Ave.
Bloomfield Hills, Missouri 48013

Newsletter of the American Magnolia Society Semiannually

The American Orchid Society
Botanical Museum of Harvard University
Cambridge, Massachusetts 02138

American Orchid Society Bulletin Monthly

American Penstemon Society
Mrs. Merle Emerson
P.O. Box 64
Somersworth, New Hampshire 03878

Bulletin Annually

American Peony Society
107½ W. Main St.
Van Wert, Ohio 45981

American Peony Society Bulletin Quarterly

The American Plant Life Society and The American Amaryllis Society Group
Dr. Thomas H. Whitaker, Exec. Sec.
P.O. Box 150
La Jolla, California 92037

Plant Life—Amaryllis Yearbook Bulletin

The American Primrose
Society
Mrs. Lawrence G. Tait,
Treas.
14015 84th Ave. NE
Bothell, Washington 98011

*Quarterly of the
American Primrose
Society*

American Rhododendron
Society
Mrs. William Curtis,
Exec. Sec.
24450 SW Grahams Ferry
Rd.
Sherwood, Oregon 97140

*The Quarterly Bulletin
of the American
Rhododendron Society*

American Rock Garden
Society
Richard W. Redfield
P.O. Box 26
Closter, New Jersey 07624

*American Rock
Garden Society
Bulletin*
Quarterly

American Rose Society
4048 Roselea Pl.
Columbus, Ohio 43214

The American Rose
Monthly

Aril Society, International
7802 Kyle St.
Sunland, California 91040

Yearbook Newsletter
3 times per year

Bonsai Clubs International
2354 Lida Dr.
Mountain View, California
94040

Bonsai Magazine 10
times per year

The Bonsai Society of
Greater New York, Inc.
P.O. Box E
Bronx, New York 10466

The Bonsai Bulletin
Quarterly

Bonsai Society of Texas
P.O. Box 11054
Dallas, Texas 75223

Bonsai Society of Texas Quarterly

Bromeliad Society
Mrs. Jeanne Woodbury
1811 Edgecliffe Dr.
Los Angeles, California
90026

The Bromeliad Journal
6 times per year

Cactus and Succulent
Society of America, Inc.
P.O. Box 167
Reseda, California 91335

Cactus and Succulent Journal Bimonthly

California Bonsai Society,
Inc.
P.O. Box 78211
Los Angeles, California
90016

Bonsai in California
Annually

California National Fuchsia
Society
Mrs. Martha Rader,
Membership Sec.
10934 E. Flory St.
Whittier, California 90606

The National Fuchsia Fan Monthly

Cymbidium Society of
America, Inc.
P.O. Box 4202
Downey, California 90242

Cymbidium Society News Monthly

Dwarf Fruit Trees Assoc.
Dept. of Horticulture
Michigan State Univ.
East Lansing, Michigan
48823

Compact Fruit Trees
Bimonthly

Dwarf Iris Society
P.O. Box 13
Middlebury, Indiana 46540

Annual Portfolio

Epiphyllum Society of
America
218 E. Greystone Ave.
Monrovia, Georgia 91016

Epiphyllum Bulletin
Irregular

The Greater New York
Orchid Society, Inc.
Mrs. Anthony DeBetta,
Corres. Sec.
116-31 Parkway Dr.
Elmont, Long Island,
New York 11003

Orchidata 6 times per
year

The Holly Society of
America, Inc.
Bluett C. Green, Jr.
P.O. Box 8445
Baltimore, Maryland 21234

Holly Letter
3 times per year

The Indoor Light Gardening
Society of America, Inc.
Mrs. Fred D. Peden, Sec.
4 Wildwood Rd.
Greenville, South Carolina
29607

Light Garden
Bimonthly

International Geranium
Society
1413 Shoreline Dr.
Santa Barbara, California
93105

*Geraniums Around the
World* Quarterly

Los Angeles International Fern Society 13715 Cordary Ave. Hawthorne, California 90250	Annual yearbook
National Chrysanthemum Society, Inc. Mrs. George S. Briggs, Sec. 8504 La Verne Dr. Adelphi, Maryland 20763	*National Chrysanthemum Society Bulletin* Quarterly
National Oleander Society 22 S. Shore Dr. Galveston, Texas 77550	*National Oleander Society* Annually
New England Wild Flower Society, Inc. Hemenway Rd. Farmingham, Massachusetts 10701	*New England Wild Flower Notes* Quarterly
North American Fruit Explorers 210 SE 108th Ave. Portland, Oregon 97216	*North American Pomona* Quarterly
North American Gladiolus Council H. Edward Frederick 234 South St. South Elgin, Illinois 60177	*NAGC Bulletin* Quarterly
North American Lily Society, Inc. Fred M. Abbey, Exec. Sec. North Ferrisburg, Vermont 05473	*Quarterly Bulletin of the North American Lily Society*

Northern Nut Growers Assoc., Inc. c/o Spencer B. Chase, Sec. 4518 Holston Hills Rd. Knoxville, Tennessee 37914	*Annual Report* *Newsletter* Quarterly
The Palm Society Mrs. Lucita H. Wait 7229 SW 54th Ave. Miami, Florida 33143	*Principes* Quarterly
Saintpaulia International P.O. Box 10604 Knoxville, Tennessee 37919	*Gesneriad Saintpaulia* *News* Bimonthly
Society for Louisiana Irises P.O. Box 175 Univ. of Southwestern Louisiana Lafayette, Louisiana 70501	*Newsletter* Quarterly

LOCAL PLANT SOCIETIES

The plant societies just listed are national organizations with headquarters in specific areas (perhaps out of your area). Some societies have branches or affiliate societies in local cities.

These organizations hold meetings once a month or so (depending on the society), at which information is exchanged and lectures on your favorite plants are given by authorities on the subject. The local meetings include plant tables—that is, plants contributed by members for a low price or sometimes for nothing; many times people have extra plants and want to share or exchange.

You do not have to be a member of the national

society to become a member of the affiliated city society. Each affiliate carries its own events and displays, shows, and lectures. Because there are so many of these shows through the year it is impossible to list them, but garden magazines such as *Flower and Garden* and *Horticulture* provide monthly lists.

GARDEN CLUBS

Garden clubs have sponsored memberships, and all states have their own member clubs. Like the plant societies, these clubs have their own publications and a nominal yearly fee. They put together exhibits for flower shows and exchange ideas about a multitude of plants. Members bring their plants for exhibit and devote both their time and effort to civic beauty and conservation.

The information is not as specific as for plant societies, but these clubs are invaluable, and devotees number into the thousands.

LIST OF GARDEN CLUB ASSOCIATIONS

Garden Club of America
598 Madison Ave.
New York, New York 10022

The Garden Club of America Bulletin 5 times per year

The Garden Club of Virginia
c/o Mrs. George H. Flowers
37 Chatham Sq.
Richmond, Virginia 23226

GCVA Journal Bimonthly

The Herb Society of
America
300 Massachusetts Ave.
Boston, Massachusetts
02115

*The Herbarist—Primer
for Herb Growing*
Annually

Men's Garden Clubs of
America
5560 Merle Hay Rd.
Des Moines, Iowa 50323

The Gardener
Bimonthly

National Council of State
Garden Clubs, Inc.
4401 Magnolia Ave.
St. Louis, Missouri 63110

The National Gardener
Bimonthly

Ohio Association of Garden
Clubs, Inc.
Mrs. Dossey Bumgarner
Rt. 2
Circleville, Ohio 43113

Garden Path
Bimonthly

Woman's National Farm
and Garden Assoc., Inc.
Mrs. Frederick G. Garrison
8200 E. Jefferson Ave.
Detroit, Michigan 48214

*The Woman's National
Magazine* Quarterly

HORTICULTURAL SOCIETIES

Many cities have what is known as horticultural
societies, which are different from plant societies,
garden clubs, and their offshoots. Horticultural societies are large organizations with somewhat higher
membership dues than the other groups. The advantage is that each society has programs and offers

16. Some garden clubs and horticultural societies maintain their own greenhouses where you can see plants and gather information. (PHOTO BY MATTHEW BARR)

service, education, and library facilities to people interested in plants. These societies also have permanent field grounds. The Chicago Horticultural Society is a fine example; lectures and outings are arranged, and a splendid program of gardening events is provided throughout the year. Some of these major organizations are affiliated with conservatories in their city, such as the Denver Botanic Gardens and Brooklyn Botanic Gardens.

For city dwellers who complain they cannot get close to nature, the horticultural societies are the answer because they provide nature for the urban person, and yearly fees are small in comparison with the wonderful programs offered. Write or call your local horticultural society for information about their activities.

The following is a list of horticultural societies. I have given the names of publications available from a few.

LIST OF HORTICULTURAL SOCIETIES

The American Horticultural Society
Mount Vernon, Virginia, 22121
Publishes *News & Views*
Quarterly

Arkansas State Horticultural Society
Univ. Of Arkansas
Room 310 Ag. Bldg.
Fayetteville, Arkansas 72701

California Horticultural Society
c/o California Academy of Sciences
Golden Gate Park
San Francisco, California 94118

Southern California Horticultural
Institute
647 S. Saltair Ave.
Los Angeles, California 90049

Western Colorado Horticultural Society
P.O. Box 587
Palisade, Colorado 81526

Connecticut Horticultural Society
199 Griswold Rd.
Wethersfield, Connecticut 06109

Peninsula Horticultural Society
145 Ag. Hall
University of Delaware
Newark, Delaware 19711

Florida State Horticultural Society
P.O. Box 552
Lake Alfred, Florida 33850
Publishes *Proceedings of the
Florida State Horticultural
Society*

Horticulture Study Society of Florida
3280 S. Miami Ave.
Miami, Florida 33129

Albany Horticultural Society
1605 Orchard Dr.
Albany, Georgia 31705

Georgia Horticultural Society, Inc.
116 Sandra Ave.
Warner Robins, Georgia 31093

Chicago Horticultural Society and Botanic
Garden
Room 402
116 S. Michigan Ave.
Chicago, Illinois 60603
Publishes *Garden Talk* Bimonthly

Indiana Horticultural Society
Dept. of Horticulture
Purdue Univ.
Lafayette, Indiana 47907

Iowa State Horticulture Society
State House
Des Moines, Iowa 50319

Kansas State Horticultural Society
Waters Hall
Manhatten, Kansas 66502

Kentucky State Horticultural Society
Ext. Horticulturist
West Kentucky Substation
Princeton, Kentucky 42445

Louisiana Horticulture Society
Lafayette, Louisiana 70501

Horticultural Society of Maryland
c/o Frederick van Hogendorp
114 W. Melrose Ave.
Baltimore, Maryland 21210

Maryland State Horticultural Society
Ext. Horticultural Specialist
Univ. of Maryland
College Park, Maryland 20740

Massachusetts Horticultural Society
300 Massachusetts Ave.
Boston, Massachusetts 02115
Publishes *Horticulture* Monthly
Nasturtium Monthly newsletter

Worcester County Horticultural Society
30 Elm St.
Worcester, Massachusetts 01608

Michigan Horticultural Society
The White House, Belle Isle
Detroit, Michigan 48207

Michigan State Horticultural Society
Michigan State Univ.
East Lansing, Michigan 48823

Minnesota State Horticultural Society
St. Paul Campus
Univ. of Minnesota
St. Paul, Minnesota 55101
Publishes *Minnesota Horticulturist*
Magazine

Missouri State Horticultural Society
P.O. Box 417
Columbia, Missouri 65201

Nebraska Horticultural Society
1739 S. 49th St.
Lincoln, Nebraska 68506

New Hampshire Horticultural Society
c/o Roy Howard
State Office Annex
Concord, New Hampshire 03300

Garden State Horticultural Association
c/o W. B. Johnson
Blake Hall
College of Agriculture & Environmental
Science
New Brunswick, New Jersey 08903

New Jersey State Horticultural Society
c/o Norman F. Childers
Rutgers The State Univ.
Horticulture & Forestry Dept.
New Brunswick, New Jersey 08903

Horticultural Society of New York
128 W. 58 St.
New York, New York 10019
Publishes *The Bulletin* Bimonthly

New York State Horticultural Society
145 Beresford Rd.
Rochester, New York 14610

North Shore Horticultural Society of Long
Island
P.O. Box 328
Glen Cove
Long Island, New York 11542

North Dakota State Horticultural Society
State Univ. Station
Fargo, North Dakota 58102

Ohio State Horticultural Society
151 Chaucer Ct.
Worthington, Ohio 43085

Blue Mountain Horticultural Society
Rt. 2, P.O. Box 348
Milton-Freewater, Oregon 97862

Oregon Horticultural Society
236 Cordley Hall
Oregon State Univ.
Corvallis, Oregon 97331

Pennsylvania Horticultural Society, Inc.
Independence National Historical Park
325 Walnut St.
Philadelphia, Pennsylvania 19106
Publishes *PHS News* Monthly
Gardeners Guide Annually

State Horticultural Association of
Pennsylvania
Loganville, Pennsylvania 17403

South Dakota State Horticultural Society
414 Tenth St.
Brookings, South Dakota 57006

Garden Club Center of the Horticultural
Society of Davidson County
Sears, Roebuck & Co.
639 Lafayette St.
Nashville, Tennessee 37203

Tennessee State Horticultural Society
Univ. of Tennessee
P.O. Box 1071
Knoxville, Tennessee 37901

Rio Grande Valley Horticultural Society
P.O. Box 107
Weslaco, Texas 78596

Utah State Horticultural Society
1750 S. Redwood Rd.
Salt Lake City, Utah 84104

Vermont State Horticultural Society
Dept. of Plant & Soil Science
Univ. of Vermont
c/o C. Lyman Calahan
Ext. Horticulturist
Burlington, Vermont 05401

Hampton Roads Horticultural Society
Box 251-A, Maxwell Lane
Newport News, Virginia 23606

Virginia State Horticultural Society
P.O. Box 718
Staunton, Virginia 24401

West Virginia State Horticultural Society
P.O. Box 592
Charles Town, West Virginia 25414

FLOWER SHOWS

Most of us are probably aware of the large spring flower shows in March in various cities like Chicago and Philadelphia. There are also local shows sponsored by horticultural organizations in specific states. These shows have admission charges, but they are worth the price because of the wealth of information and exhibits. In addition, specific plant societies such as the Orchid Society and African Violet Society have their own shows throughout the country at specified times of the year. Indeed, as you can see from this chapter, gardening goes on throughout the year at a zealous pace.

The International Flower Shows—the very big ones—are the only ones I would advise against, mainly because of admission charges, which now can cost as

17. Flower shows are held throughout the country at seasonal times and may specialize in a few kinds of flowers and plants or a wide variety of plants. Check local newspapers and garden magazines for these shows. (PHOTO BY JOYCE R. WILSON)

much as $3 per person. There is a great variety of plant material to see, but I object strongly to the number of products being sold at these shows. Many times the products have no relation to gardening at all; manufacturers, ever on the alert for places to merchandise their wares, will enter and be granted permission to exhibit. Picture-frame manufacturers or incense dealers and assorted food products such as sausage and cheese have no relation to gardening and do not belong in these floral shows.

On the other hand, the county or local flower shows, where admission is usually 50 cents, are extremely worthwhile. Here is where you will find the local plant enthusiast and clubs exhibiting their plants; these are 100 percent plant people, and they show some of the finest specimen plants you will ever see under one roof. Furthermore, there are qualified people in almost any plant division to answer questions that you may have, and commercialism is entirely absent—as it should be. Do attend these county or local shows because you will be getting a valuable education in all kinds of indoor and outdoor plants at practically no cost.

CHAPTER 5

5

CONSERVATORIES, ARBORETUMS, AND PUBLIC GARDENS

Conservatories, arboretums, and public gardens are located throughout the United States. Generally a conservatory is a large greenhouse where indoor tropical plants are grown; it is usually part of a public park. An arboretum is an outdoor garden acreage of native plants and trees or special plantings like cacti or rhododendrons. Public gardens are usually (but not always) privately owned grounds donated or maintained by various means, and there is generally an admission charge. All these places are treasure houses of beauty and provide an education for any child or gardener.

Many colleges have experimental greenhouses. I remember using the facilities of the University of Illinois for studying plants when I attended school

18. Conservatories are located in many large cities. This is Golden Gate Park Conservatory in San Francisco which houses a large number of various plants. Special shows are held at seasonal times. (PHOTO BY MATTHEW BARR)

there. The University of California has an impressive display of greenhouse plants as well as outdoor areas with hundreds of species of plants. The admission is free, and the facilities are open to the public. However, most colleges generally do *not* allow the public to view their greenhouses and experimental gardens, so phone before you go.

CONSERVATORIES

The dome conservatories of St. Louis, Houston, and Milwaukee have always been a learning ground for me, and whenever I am in these cities I spend hours (for 50 cents) under these glass domes. (My book on terrariums, *Gardens under Glass*, was partially inspired by conservatories.)

The Climatron in St. Louis simulates native environments—highly humid in one house, cool in another (depending on the plants being grown). The water lily exhibit at the entrance of the Climatron is especially worthwhile and a sight to behold in summer. Mitchell Gardens in Milwaukee has three separate domes: one for tropical plants, one for desert plants, and one for cool-growing species. These are incredible plant worlds and well worth a trip to see.

When you go through a conservatory, observe *how* the plants are grown as well as the plants themselves. Make mental note of the particular conditions where specific plants grow; this gives you the key to their successful culture. For example, note that philodendrons are generally grown in hot, humid areas. Seek out the orchids and bromeliads and other plants and get to know them. Name tags abound; the information is all there for the taking. Various employees of

19. Colleges too maintain experimental greenhouses; this is San Francisco State University College. (PHOTO BY MATTHEW BARR)

20. College greenhouses contain a wide variety of plants; some greenhouses will allow visitors, others will not, so check before you go. (PHOTO BY MATTHEW BARR)

the many conservatories throughout the United States are well schooled and will gladly answer any of your questions.

At seasonal times most conservatories have flower shows. The majority also feature book shops or nooks where you can purchase inexpensive brochures and other pertinent publications about your favorite plants.

Following is a list of conservatories that I have seen. (Many of the public gardens mentioned later also will have plants under glass as their display.) Check conservatories for days of operation and admission fees.

LIST OF CONSERVATORIES

Denver Botanic Gardens
909 York St.
Denver, Colorado 80206

Pinetum, roses, lilacs, ferns, crabapples, perennials

U.S. Botanic Garden
Conservatory
Maryland Ave. between 1st
& 2nd Sts. SW;
Office: 1st & Canal Sts. SW
Washington, DC 20024

Tropical and subtropical plants; orchids

Miami Beach Garden
Center & Conservatory
2000 Garden Center Dr.
Miami Beach, Florida 33134

Tropical plants of many kinds; orchids

Garfield Park Conservatory
300 N. Central Park
Chicago, Illinois 60624

4.5 acres of conservatories

Lincoln Park Conservatory 2400 N. Stockton Dr. Chicago, Illinois 60614	3 acres of conservatories
Berkshire Garden Center, Inc. Stockbridge, Massachusetts 01262	15-acre garden; greenhouse, indoor displays; cuttings
Anna Scripps Whitcomb Conservatory Belle Isle Detroit, Michigan 48207	Palms, cactus, ferns, orchids
Como Park Conservatory 1224 N. Lexington Pkwy. St. Paul, Minnesota 55103	Tropical plants, trees, flower displays
Missouri Botanical Garden 2315 Tower Grove Ave. St. Louis, Missouri 63110	Climatron; orchids, tropical plants, succulents
Brooklyn Botanic Gardens 1000 Washington Ave. Brooklyn, New York 11225	Roses, water lilies, hardy trees and shrubs, rhododendrons, bonsai; special gardens
Eden Park (Krohn) Conservatory Cincinnati Park Board Cincinnati, Ohio 45201	Tropical trees and shrubs, palms, ferns, cacti, aroids, succulents
Phipps Conservatory Schenley Park Pittsburgh, Pennsylvania 15213	Good display of all kinds of plants

Mitchell Pk. Conservatory
524 S. Layton Blvd.
Milwaukee, Wisconsin
53233

Three domes with
separate environments;
fine cacti and tropical
plant displays

ARBORETUMS

Arboretums are where you will find all your
outdoor plant materials such as trees and shrubs
growing profusely. For example, the arboretum in
Lisle, Illinois is an educational experience where you
can spend many, many hours observing plants.
California's Golden Gate Park boasts a collection of
native plants that is absolutely outstanding. Calloway
Gardens of Georgia is world-famous. These outdoor
plant lands are extensive and immensely educational—
a gardener's delight. Following is a list of major
arboretums.

LIST OF ARBORETUMS

Arboretum of the Univ.
of Alabama
P.O. Box 1927
Tuscaloosa, Alabama 35486

Woody plants native to
southeast United
States

Auburn Arboretum
Auburn Univ. (formerly
Alabama Polytechnic
Institute)
Auburn, Alabama 36830

In early stages of
planting

21. Arboretums contain a world of plants for the viewer, and you can spend a pleasant afternoon strolling the grounds. (PHOTO BY MATTHEW BARR)

Boyce Thompson Southwestern Arboretum P.O. Box 307 Superior, Arizona 85273	30 acres
Botanic Garden, Univ. of California Los Angeles, California 90054	Acacia, eucalyptus, callistemon, succulents
C. M. Goethe Arboretum Sacramento State College 6000 Jay St. Sacramento, California 95819	Native trees and shrubs
Irvine Arboretum Univ. of California Irvine, California 92664	Orchids, succulents, roses, citrus
Los Angeles State and County Arboretum 301 N. Baldwin Ave. Arcadia, California 91006	Exotic tropical and subtropical plants
Strybing Arboretum and Botanical Gardens Golden Gate Park San Francisco, California 94122	Rhododendrons, magnolias, dwarf conifers, native plants
Bartlett Arboretum of the State of Connecticut 151 Brookdale Rd. Stamford, Connecticut 06903	Dwarf conifers, ericaceae, yellow and purple foliage plants

22. A gazebo in the Strybing Arboretum in San Francisco, California. (PHOTO BY MATTHEW BARR)

Connecticut Arboretum at Connecticut College Connecticut College P.O. Box 1511 New London, Connecticut 06320	Native woody plants of northeast United States
U.S. National Arboretum Washington, DC 20250	Azaleas, dwarf conifers, camellia, hibiscus, ilex, lagerstroemia, magnolia, malus, pyracantha, viburnums
Gifford Arboretum Botany Dept., Univ. of Miami Coral Gables, Florida 33134	Native plants and shrubs
Charles Huston Shattuck Arboretum College of Forestry Univ. of Idaho Moscow, Idaho 83843	Rocky Mountain native trees and shrubs
Botanic Garden of the Chicago Horticultural Society 775 Dundee Rd. P.O. Box 90 Glencoe, Illinois 60022	Vast acreage now in planting stage
Morton Arboretum Rt. 53 Lisle, Illinois 60532	Crabapples, lilacs, conifers, hedges, street trees, ground covers

Christy Woods Arboretum
Ball State Teachers College
Muncie, Indiana 47302

Wheeler orchid
collection

Hayes Regional Arboretum
801 Elks Rd.
Richmond, Indiana 47374

Native woody plants

Lilac Arboretum in Ewing
Park
McKinley Ave.
Des Moines, Iowa 50300

30 acres

Indian Hill Arboretum
Topeka, Kansas 66601

Hardwoods

Bernheim Forest
Arboretum
Clermont, Kentucky 40110

Crabapples, dogwoods,
maples, nut trees,
rhododendrons,
viburnums

Louisiana Arboretum
(Chicot Arboretum)
Drawer 1111
Baton Rouge, Louisiana
70821

Native woody plants

Alexandra Botanic
Garden & Hunnewell
Arboretum
Wellesley State College
Wellesley, Massachusetts
02101

Native and introduced
trees and shrubs

Arnold Arboretum
The Arborway
Jamaica Plain,
Massachusetts 02130

Conifers, dwarf
evergreens; malus,
forsythia, syringa,
chaenomeles, lonicera,
quercus rhododendron

Michigan Arboretum Ford Motor Co. Michigan Ave. & Southfield Rd. Dearborn, Michigan 48121	Native Michigan trees and shrubs
Nichols Arboretum Univ. of Michigan Ann Arbor, Michigan 48107	Paeonia, syringa
Slayton Arboretum Hillsdale College Hillsdale, Michigan 49242	Crabapples, syringa
Hormel Foundation Arboretum Austin, Minnesota 55912	Evergreens and woody trees
Univ. of Minnesota Landscape Arboretum Chanhassen, Minnesota 55317 Mailing address: Rt. 1, P.O. Box 132-1, Chaska, Minnesota 55318	525 acres
Gloster Arboretum Gloster, Mississippi 39638 Mailing address: c/o Frank and Sara Gladney P.O. Box 1106 Baton Rouge, Louisiana 70821	327 acres
Arbor Lodge State Park Arboretum Nebraska City, Nebraska 68410	American chestnuts; liriodendron, ginkgo

Hanover Park Arboretum Mt. Pleasant Ave. East Hanover, New Jersey 07936	8 acres
Cora Hartshorn Arboretum and Bird Sanctuary Forest Drive Short Hills, New Jersey 07078	Special exhibits, trail walks
Willowwood Arboretum of Rutgers Univ. Gladstone, New Jersey 07934	130 acres
Bayard Cutting Arboretum Great River Long Island New York 11739 Mailing address: P.O. Box 66 Oakdale, New York 11739	Conifers, rhododendron hybrids, lilacs
Thomas C. Desmond Arboretum Rt. 1 Newburgh, New York 12550	Woody vines, trees, shrubs
George Landis Arboretum Esperance, New York 12066	Woody plants, native and exotic, spring bulb garden, herbaceous and rose gardens, bonsai collection

New York Botanical
Garden
200 St., east of Webster
Ave.
Bronx Park
Bronx, New York 10458

Conifers, lilacs,
rhododendrons,
azaleas, pines, native
plant garden, rock
garden

Planting Fields Arboretum
Planting Fields Rd.
P.O. Box 58
Oyster Bay, New York 11771

Rhododendrons,
synoptic shrub garden,
camellias

Robin Hill Arboretum
Platten Rd.
Lydonville, New York
14098

Trees and shrubs

Ward Pound Ridge
Reservation,
The Meyer Arboretum
Cross River, New York
10518

Wildflower garden,
trails, trees; 4500 acres

Coker Arboretum
Univ. of North Carolina
Chapel Hill, North Carolina
27514

Woody plants of
southeastern United
States

Cox Arboretum
6733 Springboro Pike
Dayton, Ohio 45449

164 acres

Dawes Arboretum
Rt. 5
Newark, Ohio 43055

Rhododendrons,
azaleas, crabapples,
beeches, hawthorns,
Japanese garden,
cypress swamp

Holden Arboretum
9500 Sperry Rd.
Mentor, Ohio 44060

Evergreens, viburnums,
rhododendrons, malus

Mt. Airy Forest and
Arboretum
5083 Colerain Ave.
Cincinnati, Ohio 45203

1500 acres in the total
forest

Stanley M. Rowe
Arboretum
4500 Muchmore Rd.
Cincinnati, Ohio 45243

Conifers, crabapples,
dwarf garden, spring
wild flowers and bulbs

Secor Park Arboretum
Rt. 1
Berkey, Ohio 43504

Maple, ash, oak,
magnolia, evergreen
school grove

Secrest Arboretum
Ohio Agricultural Research
& Development Center
Wooster, Ohio 44691

Taxus, crabapples, firs,
spruces, junipers,
rhododendrons

R. A. Stranahan Arboretum
Univ. of Toledo
33 Birkhead Pl.
Toledo, Ohio 43606

Native woodland

Hoyt Arboretum
4000 SW Fairview Blvd.
Portland, Oregon 97221

Conifers and broadleaf
trees

Peavy Arboretum
School of Forestry, Oregon
State College
Corvallis, Oregon 97330

Native conifers

Arboretum of the Barnes Foundation 300 Latches Lane Merion Station, Pennsylvania 19066	Magnolias, lilacs, peonies, viburnums, cotoneasters, conifers, stewartia
Awbury Arboretum Washington Lane & Ardleigh St. Germantown, Pennsylvania 19152	110 species of trees and shrubs
Coover Arboretum Rt. 3 Dillsburg, Pennsylvania 17019	Native wild flowers, conifers, nut trees, boxwood, holly oak, rhododendrons
Ellis School Arboretum Newtown Square, Pennsylvania 19073	Shade and flowering trees
Hershey Rose Gardens and Arboretum Hershey, Pennsylvania 17033	1,200 varieties of roses; holly, hemerocallis, dwarf evergreens, azaleas
Morris Arboretum of the Univ. of Pennsylvania Rt. 422, Chestnut Hill Philadelphia, Pennsylvania 19118 Mailing address: 9414 Meadowbrook Ave. Philadelphia, Pennsylvania 19118	Roses, hollies, ivy, azaleas, rhododendrons, magnolias, dogwoods

Taylor Memorial Arboretum 10 Ridley Dr. Garden City Chester, Pennsylvania 19013	Heather, cotoneaster, boxwood
John J. Tyler (Painter) Arboretum 515 Painter Rd., P.O. Box 216 Lima, Pennsylvania 19060	Specimen trees, rhododendrons, dogwoods, fragrant garden, conifers
Westtown School Arboretum Westtown, Pennsylvania 19315	Conifers
Meadowby Arboretum and Nursery, RD 1 Lewisburg, Pennsylvania 17837	Rhododendrons, pines, lilacs, magnolias, viburnums
Southwestern Arboretum Southwestern College of Memphis Memphis, Tennessee 38117	Native woody species
Univ. of Tennessee Arboretum 901 Kerr Hollow Rd. Oak Ridge, Tennessee 37830	Pinus, ilex, native plants
Lubbock Municipal Garden & Arts Center, Inc. Lubbock Memorial Arboretum Foundation, Inc. 4215 University Ave. Lubbock, Texas 79413	90-acre park

State Arboretum of Utah Univ. of Utah, Bldg. 306 Salt Lake City, Utah 84112	Hybrid oaks, native and exotic conifers, roses, herbs, opuntia, sequoiadendron
Orland E. White Research Arboretum Univ. of Virginia Boyce, Virginia 22628	140 acres
Tech Mountain Trails Arboretum Dept. of Botany West Virginia Institute of Technology Montgomery, West Virginia 25136	Natural mixed mesophytic forest at 600 to 1700-foot elevation
West Virginia Univ. Arboretum Dept. of Biology West Virginia Univ. Morgantown, West Virginia 26506	Native wild flowers, shrubs, woody plants
Paine Art Center & Arboretum P.O. Box 1097 Oshkosh, Wisconsin 54901	Dwarf lilacs, evergreens, eighteenth century English flower garden
Univ. of Wisconsin Arboretum 1207 Seminole Hwy. Madison, Wisconsin 53711	Lilacs, crabapples, viburnums, native plants, small shrub display

PUBLIC GARDENS

These masterpieces of landscaped plants and art are open to the public at almost all times of the year, depending on the individual garden and climate. Generally there is a nominal admission charge, but it is well worth the price of entrance because of the unbelievable amount of plant knowledge available and the landscaped grounds. Many also have display greenhouses. Once again, call for hours and admission fees (if any).

LIST OF PUBLIC GARDENS

Bellingrath Gardens
Theodore, Alabama 36582

800 acres; 65 are landscaped

Arizona-Sonora Desert Museum and Demonstration Garden
P.O. Box 5607,
Tucson Mt. Park
Tucson, Arizona 85703

Native plants of Sonora Desert

Descanso Gardens
Dept. of Arboreta and Botanic Gardens
1418 Descanso Dr.
La Canada, California 91011

Camellias, azaleas, roses, native plants

Golden Gate Park
San Francisco, California 94122

Rhododendrons, rose garden, Japanese Tea Garden, garden for the blind in arboretum

Huntington Botanical Gardens 1151 Oxford Rd. San Marino, California 91108	Camellias, cactus, Japanese Garden, conifers, palms
South Coast Botanic Garden 26701 Rolling Hills Rd. Palos Verdes Peninsula California 90274	87 acres
Univ. of California Botanic Gardens School of Biological and Agricultural Sciences Univ. of California Riverside, California 92502	37 acres
Winterthur Gardens Winterthur, Delaware 19735	Azaleas, rhododendrons, conifers, bulbs
Dumbarton Oaks 1703 32nd St. NW Washington, District of Columbia 20007	Roses, chrysanthemums, herbaceous borders
Kenilworth Aquatic Gardens Douglas St. NE Washington, DC 20250	Water lilies, native pond, marsh and riverbank plants
Fairchild Tropical Garden 10901 Old Cutler Rd. Miami, Florida 33156	Palms, cycads

Villa Viscaya Dade County Park Department Miami, Florida 33100	10 acres; Italian gardens
Callaway Gardens Pine Mountain, Georgia 31822	Azaleas, hollies, quinces, crabapples, magnolias, dogwoods
James Irving Holcomb Botanical Garden, Butler Univ. Indianapolis, Indiana 46200	Lilac, holly euonymus, annuals, perennials
Honeywell Gardens P.O. Box 432 Wabash, Indiana 46992	Roses, Indiana native hardwoods
Hodges Garden P.O. Box 921 Many, Louisiana 71449	Aroids, gesneriads, euphorbias, roses, amaryllis, orchids
Longue Vue Gardens 7 Bamboo Rd. New Orleans, Louisiana 70124	8 acres
Fay Hyland Botanical Plantation 371 Deering Hall Univ. of Maine Orono, Maine 04473	Native plants
Thuya Gardens Asticou Terrace Northeast Harbor, Maine 04662	Herbaceous border, natural plantings

Boston Public Garden Boston, Massachusetts 02101	Formal gardens, rare trees
Eloise Butler Wild Flower Garden and Bird Sanctuary c/o Board of Park Commissioners 250 S. Fourth St. Minneapolis, Minnesota 55415	Native plants
Cedar Brook Park Union County Park System Plainfield, New Jersey 07061	Irises, daffodils, daylilies, peonies, dogwoods, Shakespeare Garden
Duke Gardens Foundation, Inc. Rt. 206 South Somerville, New Jersey 08876	Ornamental flowering plants and tropicals under glass
Carlsbad Botanical and Zoological Park Carlsbad, New Mexico 88220	Desert plants
Bartow-Pell Mansion, Museum and Gardens Shore Rd. Pelham Bay Park Bronx, New York 10464	Formal gardens, woodland, rhododendron walk
Central Park 59th St. to 110th St. New York, New York	Seasonal displays at Conservatory Gardens

Old Westbury Gardens P.O. Box 265 Old Westbury Rd. Old Westbury, New York 11568	Flowering shrubs and trees; perennials of recent hybrid origin
Reader's Digest Gardens Pleasantville, New York 10570	Spring floral displays
Sterling Forest Gardens P.O. Box 608 Tuxedo, New York 10987	Floral displays, woodland
Clarendon Gardens Linden Rd. Pinehurst, North Carolina 28374	Hollies, azaleas, camellias, hybrid rhododendrons
Reynolda Gardens Wake Forest Univ. P.O. Box 7325, Reynolda Station Winston-Salem, North Carolina 27109	Magnolias, junipers, hemerocallis, native trees, Japanese flowering cherries
Gardenview Horticultural Park 16711 Pearl Rd. Strongsville, Ohio 44136	Trees, perennials, unusual and uncommon shrubs; 500 varieties of flowering crabapples
Will Rogers Horticulture Garden Will Rogers Park 3500 NW 36 St. Oklahoma City, Oklahoma 73112	Roses, hibiscus, lagerstroemia, irises, junipers, hollies

Longwood Gardens Kennett Square, Pennsylvania 19348	Orchids, camellias, azaleas, large trees, tropical and subtropical ornamentals
Brookgreen Gardens Murrells Inlet, South Carolina 39576	Indigenous oaks and hollies
Cypress Gardens Charleston, South Carolina 29404	Azaleas, camellias
Magnolia Gardens Charleston, South Carolina 29404	Azaleas, camellias, magnolias
Memphis Botanic Garden Audubon Park 750 Cherry Rd. Memphis, Tennessee 38117	Trees, shrubs, herbaceous plants, roses
Dallas Garden Center Forest & First St. State Fair Grounds, P.O. Box 26194 Dallas, Texas 75226	Educational programs, shows
San Antonio Garden Center, Inc. 3310 N. New Braunfels Ave. San Antonio, Texas 78209	Flower shows, spring garden schools
Colonial Williamsburg P.O. Box C Williamsburg, Virginia 23185	Eighteenth century gardens

Norfolk Botanical Garden
Airport Rd.
Norfolk, Virginia 23518

Azaleas,
rhododendrons, roses,
camellias, hollies,
Japanese, colonial,
blind (fragrance)
gardens

Alfred L. Boerner Botanical
Gardens
5879 S. 92nd St.
Hales Corners, Wisconsin
53130

Pinetum crabapples,
lilacs, bulbs, roses,
dwarf fruit trees,
peonies, annuals,
perennials

6

HELP FOR FREE

No matter what garden problem you have, and no matter how hopeless it seems, there is free and expert information to help you combat the problem—if you know where to find it. Whether you are fighting an aphid infestation on your favorite rose or rust on the gladiolas, there are government agencies—the United States Department of Agriculture (USDA), Agricultural Extension Services, and United States Forestry Service—to help you help your plants.

There is also help for your plants at your local nursery. However, I have found through the years that you must select the *right* nursery, with *qualified* people who can answer your gardening questions, because in many places help and advice are transient. Most owners of small nurseries are well-qualified people who know the plants of their district—what will and will not grow. These are valuable people to go to, and invariably they will take the time to answer your questions. Indeed, they will often volunteer information when you buy.

VARIOUS GOVERNMENT SERVICES

The various government services lead the list of useful suppliers of information about everything from Agaves to Zantedeschias. This bounty of knowledge is at your fingertips: a phone call or a postage stamp away. Do not expect quick replies or catered humbleness from these services, but if you are reasonably patient you will have your questions answered, and free or minimum-cost pamphlets about specific subjects will be sent on request.

As with all bureaucracy, there are levels of authority. Don't give up before you start. Often, if you start within your own state, you will not have to go any further. Some of the government agricultural services are listed in your local phone book under County Agency, County Extension Service and Soil Conservation Service, Forestry Division, and son on. (For USDA, look under the United States Government listings in your local phone book.) If these people cannot help you, they will tell you who can. Be explicit, have definite questions, and do not bother these services unduly. Remember, they are generally under-staffed and extremely busy. However, also remember that you are paying their salaries, so learn how to use them to your benefit. Working within the system does have its benefits if you know how to do it. If you have insect problems in your garden, do not run to your local nursery and buy endless remedies. They are not necessary and they cost money. Call your county agent and explain the situation. He will try to identify the insect if you send it and tell you what to do to combat it. If your trees are dying for no reason, go to the phone again; call the county agent and ask him if some blight or insect has invaded the area. He will advise you just how to proceed.

In addition to your county and state helpers there is the federal government, the largest source of published gardening information. The address for their list of publications (45 cents) is: United States Department of Agriculture, Superintendent of Documents, U.S. Government Printing Office, Washington, DC. The USDA offers pamphlets, booklets, and hardcover books dealing with plant diseases, seeds, trees—an array of gardening subjects. The pamphlets are clear, concise, and reasonably priced: 20, 35, and 40 cents. (The definitive books about special subjects cost $3. This material may be heavy reading and not full of glorified pictures, but within these books is solid information written by experts in the field.)

Some large cities (for example, New York, San Francisco, and Chicago) have central offices for the federal government publications. You can buy their booklets and books covering various aspects of gardening and land, thereby eliminating the letter-writing and postage cost. These city offices and their addresses are:

Government Printing Office
710 North Capitol St.
Washington, DC 20402

The Pentagon
Main Concourse,
South End
Washington, DC
20310

Department of Commerce,
Lobby
14th and Constitution Ave.
NW
Washington, DC 20230

USIA Building, 1st Floor
1776 Pennsylvania Ave.
NW
Washington, DC 20547

Department of State
Building, 1st Floor
2201 C St. NW
Washington, DC 20520

Room 1C46
Federal Building, U.S.
Courthouse
1100 Commerce St.
Dallas, Texas 75202

Room 1421
Federal Building, U.S.
Courthouse
1961 Stout St.
Denver, Colorado 80202

Room 135, Federal
Office Building
601 East 12th St.
Kansas City, Missouri 64106

Room 100, Federal
Building
275 Peachtree St. NE
Atlanta, Georgia
30303

Room G25, J F K
Federal Building
Sudbury St.
Boston,
Massachusetts 02203

Room 1463, 14th Floor
Everett M. Dirksen
Building
219 South Dearborn St.
Chicago, Illinois
60604

Room 1015,
Federal Office
Building
300 North Los
Angeles St.
Los Angeles,
California 90012

Room 110,
Federal Office
Building
26 Federal Plaza
New York,
New York 10007

Room 1023, Federal
Office Building
450 Golden Gate Ave.
San Francisco,
California 94102

The United States Government, as mentioned, supplies a list of all their publications for 45 cents. From this master list you select the price list (and titles) of gardening subjects that interest you. These lists are free; I keep the following on hand:

PL 35 *National Parks*   PL 44 *Plants*
PL 41 *Insects*   PL 46 *Soils and Fertilizers*
PL 43 *Forestry*   PL 88 *Ecology*

In addition to the above subject booklets, new subject listings are issued about twice a month. The twice-monthly listings (called *Selected U.S. Government Publications*), about popular and new subjects, are free on request. Write for this selected list to: Public Documents Distribution Center, Pueblo, Colorado 81009.

From the 45-cent Price List, here are some pamphlets available. Most are priced from 10 to 25 cents. To order, write to the Superintendent of Documents, U.S. Government Printing Office, Washington, D.C. 20404. Supplies are limited and prices are subject to change without notice.

2J   *Grass Varieties in the U.S.*, no publication date listed

3J   *Shade Trees for The Home*, no publication date listed

31J   *Chemical Control of Plant Growth*, no publication date listed

48K   *Color It Green with Trees*, no publication date listed

49K   *Growing Azaleas and Rhododendrons*, no publication date listed

G71   *Growing Azaleas and Rhododendrons*, 1970

G25 *Roses for the Home,* 1970
G82 *Selecting and Growing House Plants,* 1963
G89 *Selecting Fertilizers for Lawns and Gardens,* 1971
G142 *Selecting Shrubs for Shady Areas,* 1970
T1291 *Seven Species of Broadleaf Deciduous Trees for Windbreaks—Effect of Spacing Distance and Age on Their Survival and Growth at Cheyenne, Wyoming,* 1963
G136 *Spring Flowering Bulbs,* 1971
G151 *Summer Flowering Bulbs,* 1971

In addition to the above fine publications, there is also a list of yearbooks from the USDA that is worth its weight in gold; the list includes:

Seeds, Yearbook of Agriculture, 1961 ($3.50)

Plant Diseases, Yearbook of Agriculture, 1953 ($3.50)

Landscape For Living, Yearbook of Agriculture, 1972 ($3.50)

On request from the local government printing office in your city (listed previously) or from Superintendent of Documents, U.S. Government Printing Office, Washington, DC 20402, you can receive the list of yearbooks free.

Another publication of the United States Government Printing Office is a special *Home Garden Brochure,* which you should have. This is available from the Public Documents Distribution Service Center, 5801 Tabor Ave., Philadelphia, Pennsylvania 19120, and offers a variety of pamphlets about gardening. Following is a résumé: Prices vary from 10 to 30 cents. Supplies are limited and prices are subject to change without notice.

1. *Better Lawns*
2. *How to Buy Lawn Seed*
3. *Lawn Weeds Control with Herbicides*
4. *Growing Camellias*
5. *Growing Flowering Annuals*
6. *Growing the Flowering Dogwood*
7. *Growing Vegetables in the Home Garden*
8. *Trees for Shade and Privacy*
9. *Selecting Shrubs for Shady Areas*
10. *Transplanting Ornamental Trees and Shrubs*
11. *Shrubs, Vines and Trees for Summer Color*
12. *Growing Tomatoes in the Home Garden*
13. *Growing Ornamentals in Urban Gardens*
14. *Growing Flowering Perennials*
15. *Growing Ground Covers*
16. *Ants in the Home Garden and How to Control Them*
17. *Roses for the Home*
18. *Mulches for Your Garden*
19. *Minigardens for Vegetables*
20. *Shade Trees for the Home*

As you can see from the above list, there are helpful booklets about almost every garden subject. Although the booklets are not definitive (some are only eight pages long), there is enough valid information to get you started in the right direction. Prices, you will note, are certainly low for the amount of information given.

Order well ahead of time because supply is limited and publications are sent by fourth-class book rate mail, which takes several weeks.

Thus, even with a very minimum expenditure, the

gardener can accumulate a very good, inexpensive garden library to help him help his plants. Once you have some knowledge of the gardening scene and about specific plants—trees, shrubs, vegetables—you can purchase regular garden books. In other words, you will have some idea of what you want, and will spend your money wisely.

For the most part we have concentrated on gardening on a small scale, but the United States Government also offers publications for those interested in commercial gardening and farming; such as setting up an orchard, running a small farm, and so on. Upon written request and receipt of nominal charge, the USDA will also supply you with maps of your area. These maps indicate yearly rainfall, first frosts, and other pertinent weather information. They

23. Maps of both frost dates and precipitation are available from the United States Department of Agriculture on request. This map shows average dates of last killing frost in spring for the United States. (USDA PHOTO)

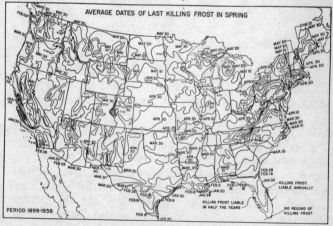

can help you greatly in determining your weather growing conditions, especially if you are new in the area. Remember, the plants you grow are more or less governed by climate, which includes rainfall and temperature. These maps can save you needless worry in determining the kinds of plants for your garden.

UNITED STATES FORESTRY SERVICE

This is still another facet of the USDA that deals specifically with trees. Most of their publications are geared to growing trees on the commercial levels, but they also have a few publications for the home owner, with more to come. One of their latest free booklets is *People, Cities and Trees.* Of special interest is their publication Research Bulletin 246, *Trees and Shrubs for Noise Abatement*, a veritable treasure house of information prepared by the Forest Division of the USDA in cooperation with the University of Nebraska College of Agriculture.

Also available from the Forestry Division is a listing of seedling trees you can buy at nominal cost. The minimum order is 100 trees, but you can buy, for example, Austrian pines, 4 to 10 inches tall, at $36.50/100. If five home owners get together, each can have 20 trees for about $9, or less than 50 cents per tree!

A final service from the USDA (without going into farm-help publications and divisions) is the Soil Conservation Service, which will give technical assistance to individuals to help improve the use of land and water resources. The service works with local conservation groups, and is listed under the United States Government heading in your local phone book.

OTHER PUBLICATIONS

Before we leave free or minimal cost pamphlets, brochures, and books, I want to mention the fine publications offered by the Brooklyn Botanic Gardens. These handbooks are reasonably priced and offer solid information about various gardening subjects. They are not the final answer, but they certainly are an excellent start to get you gardening.

These horticultural handbooks range from 64 to 112 pages, are prepared by experts, and can be ordered by name or number from Brooklyn Botanic Gardens, 1000 Washington Avenue, Brooklyn, New York 11225. Here is a brief list of some of their booklets (all cost $1):

#20	*Soils*
#21	*Lawns*
#25	*100 Finest Trees and Shrubs*
#26	*Gardening in Containers*
#34	*Biological Control of Plant Pests*
#40	*House Plants*
#48	*Roses*
#49	*Creative Ideas in Garden Design*

AGRICULTURAL EXTENSION SERVICE

As a taxpayer, your Extension Service is your private answering advisory tool. Questions about raising plants, pest fighting, and soil can be answered here. Address letters (and be specific about questions) to the following locations:

Agricultural Information
Auburn Univ.
Auburn, Alabama 36830

Agricultural Information
Univ. of Alaska
College, Alaska 99701

Agricultural Information
College of Agriculture
Univ. of Arizona
Tucson, Arizona 85721

Agricultural Information
Univ. of Arkansas
P.O. Box 391
Little Rock, Arkansas
72203

Agricultural Information
Agricultural Ext. Service
2200 University Ave.
Berkeley, California
94720

Agricultural Information
Colorado State Univ.
Fort Collins, Colorado
80521

Agricultural Information
College of Agriculture
Univ. of Connecticut
Storrs, Connecticut
06268

Agricultural Information
College of Agricultural
Sciences
Univ. of Delaware
Newark, Delaware 19711

Agricultural Information
Univ. of Florida
217 Rolfs Hall
Gainesville, Florida 32601

Agricultural Information
College of Agriculture
Univ. of Georgia
Athens, Georgia 30602

Agricultural Information
Univ. of Hawaii
2500 Dole St.
Honolulu, Hawaii 96822

Agricultural Information
College of Agriculture
Univ. of Idaho
Moscow, Idaho 83843

Agricultural Information
College of Agriculture
Univ. of Illinois
Urbana, Illinois 61801

Agricultural Information
Agricultural
Administration Bldg.
Purdue Univ.
Lafayette, Indiana 47907

Agricultural Information
Iowa State Univ.
Ames, Iowa 50010

Agricultural Information
Kansas State Univ.
Manhattan, Kansas
66502

Agricultural Information
College of Agriculture
Univ. of Kentucky
Lexington, Kentucky
40506

Agricultural Information
Louisiana State Univ.
Knapp Hall, Univ.
Station
Baton Rouge, Louisiana
70803

Agricultural Information
Dept of Public
Information
Univ. of Maine
Orono, Maine 04473

Agricultural Information
Univ. Of Maryland
Agricultural Division
College Park, Maryland
20742

Agricultural Information
Stockbridge Hall
Univ. of Massachusetts
Amherst, Massachusetts
01002

Agricultural Information
Dept. of Information
Services
109 Agricultural Hall
East Lansing, Michigan
48823

Department of
Information
Institute of Agriculture
Univ. of Minnesota
St. Paul, Minnesota
55101

Agricultural Information
Mississippi State Univ.
State College,
Mississippi 39762

Agricultural Information
1-98 Agricultural Bldg.
Univ. of Missouri
Columbia, Missouri
65201

Office of Information
Montana State Univ.
Bozeman, Montana
59715

Department of
Information
College of Agriculture
Univ. of Nebraska
Lincoln, Nebraska 68503

Agricultural
Communications Service
Univ. of Nevada
Reno, Nevada 89507

Agricultural Information
Schofield Hall
Univ. of New Hampshire
Durham, New Hampshire
03824

Agricultural Information
College of Agriculture
Rutgers, The State Univ.
New Brunswick, New
Jersey 08903

Agricultural Information
Drawer 3A1
New Mexico State Univ.
Las Cruces, New Mexico
88001

Agricultural Information
State College of
Agriculture
Cornell Univ.
Ithaca, New York 13850

Agricultural Information
North Carolina State
Univ.
State College Station
Raleigh, North Carolina
27607

Agricultural Information
North Dakota State Univ.
State Univ. Station
Fargo, North Dakota
58102

Cooperative Extension
Service
The Ohio State Univ.
2120 Fyffe Road
Columbus, Ohio 43210

Agricultural Information
Oklahoma State Univ.
Stillwater, Oklahoma
74074

Agricultural Information
206 Waldo Hall
Oregon State Univ.
Corvallis, Oregon 97331

Agricultural Information
The Pennsylvania State
Univ.
Room 1, Armsby Bldg.
University Park,
Pennsylvania 16802

Cooperative Ext. Service
Univ. of Puerto Rico
Mayaguez Campus,
P.O. Box AR
Rio Piedras, Puerto Rico
00928

Agricultural Information
Univ. of Rhode Island
16 Woodwall Hall
Kingston, Rhode Island
02881

Agricultural Information
Clemson Univ.
Clemson, South Carolina
29631

Agricultural Information
South Dakota State Univ.
Univ. Station
Brookings, South Dakota
57006

Agricultural Information
Univ. of Tennessee
P.O. Box 1071
Knoxville, Tennessee
37901

Department of
Agricultural Information
Services Bldg.
Texas A & M Univ.
College Station,
Texas 77843

Agricultural Information
Utah State Univ.
Logan, Utah 84321

Agricultural Information
Univ. of Vermont
Burlington, Vermont
05401

Agricultural Information
Virginia Polytechnic
Institute
Blacksburg, Virginia
24061

Agricultural Information
115 Wilson Hall
Washington State Univ.
Pullman, Washington
99163

Agricultural Information
Evansdale Campus
Appalachian Center
West Virginia Univ.
Morgantown, West
Virginia 26506

Agricultural Information
Univ. of Wisconsin
Madison, Wisconsin
53706

Agricultural Information
Univ. of Wyoming
P.O. Box 3354
Laramie, Wyoming
82070

Information Services
Federal Ext. Service
U.S. Department of
Agriculture
Washington, DC 20250

24. Highway plantings can give you a clue as to what plants can take abuse and pollution. (PHOTO BY MATTHEW BARR)

HIGHWAY DEPARTMENT, PLANTING DIVISION

Throughout the United States, the Highway Departments maintain a planting division that supervises, selects, and plants greenery along freeways. In some states the highway plantings are extraordinarily beautiful, but in other states they are sorely lacking. Yet with proper plantings, highways need not be eyesores. Furthermore, trees and shrubs are noise barriers as well as air cleaners. Indeed, heavy plantings along freeways can and do eliminate a great deal of contaminants from the air and thus from your lungs.

If specific plants can grow along highways where pollutants are high, they can survive in almost any situation. They must be robust and tough! The Highway Department, however, is not a free answering service for your plant problems, so do not expect too much help. However, what I have done, and you can too, is to make note of plants growing along specific areas of freeways, or call and ask just what has been planted so you can follow suit in your own property. However, once again, let me remind you that the Highway Department, Planning and Planting Division is not an answering service; use it with discretion.

CONSERVATION ORGANIZATIONS

These organizations are mainly concerned with keeping the ecology intact, which is no easy chore these days. Although protection and conservation are the organization's main goals, they also are generally well schooled in soil and plant problems. One segment of nature governs another, and membership

25. Experimental forests are maintained by the United States Forestry Service. While their interest is primarily on a commercial basis they do have some information for the average gardener. (U.S. FOREST SERVICE PHOTO)

in these conservation groups will keep you abreast of the latest legislation about conservation, ecology, and related matters. By all means, if you have any questions about ecology or conservation, write and ask questions. Make yourself heard.

The American Forestry Assoc.
919 17th St. NW
Washington, DC 20006

Friends Of The Earth
30 East 42nd St.
New York, New York 10017

National Audubon Society
1130 Fifth Ave.
New York, New York 10028

National Parks and Conservation Society
1701 18th St. NW
Washington, DC 20009

The National Wildlife Federation
1412 16th St. NW
Washington, DC 20006

The Nature Conservancy
Suite 800
1800 North Kent St.
Arlington, Virginia 22209

Sierra Club
1050 Mills Tower
San Francisco, California 94104

The Wilderness Society
729 15th St. NW
Washington, DC 20005

The Izaak Walton League of America
1326 Waukegon Rd.
Glenview, Illinois 60025

7

FREE CONTAINERS AND GIFTS FROM GARBAGE

Sometimes a container for a plant can cost more than the plant itself. And in nurseries today we are tempted by a vast choice of attractive housings for plants. But you can have equally nice containers from household items such as empty coffee cans, bottles, and jars. These pots are just as nice—or can be, if you use your imagination—than a purchased container.

COFFEE CANS, OIL CANS, ETC

Coffee cans have always been fine containers for indoor plants; it takes but a few seconds to make them attractive. Punch some holes in the bottom with a nail or ice pick, and cover the outside with

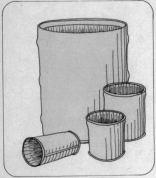

1. select planter (coffee can,
   paint can, tobacco tin,
   oil tin, etc.)

2. thoroughly clean and smooth
   surface to be painted or
   applied with contact paper

3. when applying contact paper
   always work in one direction,
   flattening air bubbles as you go

4. the finished product should be
   attractive as well as practical

Homemade Containers

decorative adhesive papers ("Contact" is available in many designs) or paint the can. Coffee cans come in three or four different sizes, so suit the plant to the pot; for example, small ones in 1-pound cans, larger plants in 2-pound cans. For a novel effect, use three cans of different heights in a group; this makes a fine indoor display area for your greenery.

Cans containing Crisco or similar products can be used in the same manner. Clean them thoroughly with soap and water. Punch holes in the bottom for drainage and then cover them with paper or paint them.

If you have large indoor plants, the many ice cream parlors throughout the country offer large empty ice cream drums that can also be fashioned into plant containers. All you have to do is ask for them at the stores, clean them, and they are yours at no charge. To make them attractive, use wood lathing around them or put them in macramé slings. Service stations and oil companies, too, will occasionally offer free drums; these are generally large, but if painted can serve as decorative outdoor containers.

BOTTLES

Wine decanters, cider jugs, and all kinds of bottles can also be used for plants. Use the new glass-cutting kits. At first you may think it is impossible to cut a bottle, but it can be done with a little practice. Bottoms of glass jugs cut midway make lovely containers for plants set on a table or inserted in a hanging basket made of macramé or burlap. And you need not stop there; the top of the bottle can be inverted over a dish and used as an inexpensive domed terrarium.

26. A glass-cutting kit will enable you to use discarded bottles for plant containers. Bottle is scored first and tapped. (PHOTO BY AUTHOR)

27. Cut bottle ready for use either as a dome for a terrarium or as a hanging container for plants. (PHOTO BY AUTHOR)

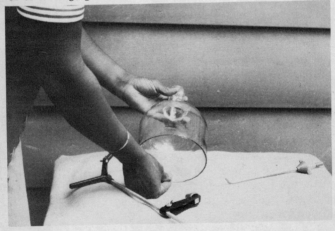

28. Cut bottle used over a terrarium arrangement. (PHOTO
BY AUTHOR)

You can also make bottle gardens simply by using two bottles to make one. For example, cut one bottle 3 inches from the bottom. Cut the second jug as close to the bottom as possible. Plant the first bottle with soil and plants, and then merely place the top half of the second jug on top. Seal the segments with epoxy.

Cutting bottles is hardly beyond the average person's ability. It does take time and patience and a few attempts, but it is one way to use otherwise wasted bottles. The expenditure for the bottle-cutting kit is $4.95 to $7.95. However, you can use an ordinary 25-cent glass cutter. It takes more time and skill, but with practice it can be done. Score the mark with a glass crayon. Run the glass cutter along the line. Make the cut deftly and quickly and without too much pressure. There should be a soft ripping sound with no skips or bumps. If the cut is white or throws chips, you are pressing too hard. Once the cut is made, soak a string or cord in lighter fluid, tie it around the cut, and then ignite the string. When the flame dies, plunge the bottle neck down into a bucket of cold water. Smooth the edges with a carborundum stone or #60 emery paper (inexpensive). Use gloves; working with glass can be hazardous.

Because bottles are thrown away anyway and many times end up smashed along the freeway or in your driveway, doesn't it make better sense to utilize your bottles to make lovely, free greeneries for viewing?

OTHER CONTAINERS

Salvage containers are other free or almost-free housings for plants. Annually, the local suitcase manufacturers offer defective plastic rectangular con-

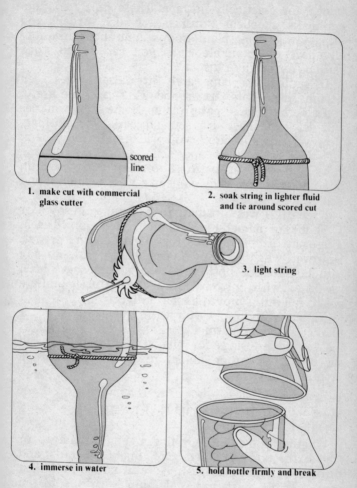

1. make cut with commercial glass cutter

2. soak string in lighter fluid and tie around scored cut

3. light string

4. immerse in water

5. hold bottle firmly and break

Cutting Bottles

tainers for practically nothing. These sturdy containers make excellent housings for dish gardens and
other low-growing plant groups. Junk shops occasionally have old concrete sinks you can use in stone
gardens for outdoor display.

Discarded tea cups and throwaway vases, can
become plant-pots. Barrel and wine casks are useful
containers for large patio plants. Some small wineries
will let you have barrels and casks for nothing.
However, in most areas you will have to buy them,
but they are still cheaper than commercially made
containers sold at patio shops. Look for them in
discount markets. They come in several diameters and
make fine containers.

Recently I was fortunate to find some old soy kegs
12 inches in diameter and 12 inches deep for $3 each.
These are excellent tubs for plants indoors or out.
However, when you buy a sawed barrel, cask or a soy
tub, be sure the bottom is sturdy; some have been
reworked with bottoms just slotted in place and are
apt to fall out if moved haphazardly.

Nature will supply you with free containers for
plants; stones and small rocks with eroded pockets
make fine housings for plants. Planted with small
succulents or other miniature plants, they are a
unique accent.

GIFTS FROM GARBAGE

Whether you call it recycling, a gift from nature, or
free-earth bounty, there are many discards and
throwaways that can become useful garden tools. Tin
cans, plastic meat trays, aluminum cartons frozen
rolls come in, and milk cartons have many uses in
gardening. These are like gifts, so use them when you
can.

Tin cans, forever present in most households, are a garbage problem. But they need not be. Small cans can be used as plant starters. Remove both the top and bottom, put the containers in plastic lids (from other large cans), and fill the small cans with soil. These will do fine for seedlings. At transplanting time, soak the soil and shake the container. The new plant will come out with a nice root ball ready for garden planting. You can also use the cans directly in the garden. Push the root and soil part-way down through the bottom of the earth, and leave the can as a metal ring around the plant. The metal wall will deter cutting insects that destroy plants, and the method of planting will encourage good root growth to spread out below the can.

You can also use large coffee and Crisco cans as an irrigation device. Remove both tops and bottoms, and sink the cans two-thirds their length into the soil near the plants that require frequent water. Put water in these canned reservoirs. The water will seep out in the direction of the plant roots; you will save time watering and scoff at droughts. Be sure the can is placed just right to ensure water runoff in the direction of the plant.

Aluminum and plastic trays and milk cartons can be put into garden service as seed starters; milk cartons can be used (with bottom and top removed) as collars for young garden plants to thwart insects— they cannot scale the slippery walls.

CHAPTER 8

8

SHORTCUTS
TO LONG SAVINGS

A good soil with adequate nutrients is the basis of a good garden. But after a few years soil is generally depleted of food for plants and must be replaced (costly) or replenished (not so costly). Soil needs turning and tilling, organic additives, and care. Did you ever wonder where the soil comes from that you buy? At one time it was relatively inexpensive. Soil contractors would make arrangements with contractors at excavation sites to remove soil, sometimes for nothing. Not so any more. Soil is becoming a scarce, increasingly expensive commodity, so you must learn to use what is on your property, adding new soil with discretion. The reasons involve more than money, mainly conservation. And because there are ways of "stretching" your soil and making it better, it makes sense to use as little new soil as possible.

SOIL

Today only the affluent gardener can afford great amounts of new soil. For example, a 6-yard truck of topsoil (enough for a 5-by-10-foot area) can cost as much as $60, depending upon where you live. Topsoil is soil that has been mixed with sand and humus (nutrients) and thoroughly screened of lumps, debris, and clods. One grade down and cheaper is the unscreened, unhumused soil. Also available from soil contractors is soil "as is," in other words, "fill" that has been excavated from building sites; it may have everything in it from stones to concrete to beer cans. This soil, however, rarely sells for more than $2 a yard and can be used if you know how to improve it. Fill must be mixed (by you) with sand and humus and all clods and debris removed by you. Still, with soil prices rocketing, this is one way to save money. It

29. Soil that is available in packages is frightfully expensive. Buy it only if you must. (PHOTO BY MATTHEW BARR)

is hard work and takes time, but eventually fill soil becomes good soil—Mother Earth renews herself, if you know how to help her along.

Packaged soil at nurseries is sold in convenient sacks of 20 or 25 pounds. But this is a frightfully expensive way to supply a garden with soil; it can break an ordinary man. Avoid it! Buy if you must the small hobby sacks for planting house plants (even this is expensive), but for any quantity buy by the truckload from building material suppliers or soil contractors.

Occasionally, and depending upon where you live, you may be able to deal directly with the companies that excavate sites. If you can, do so! Prices are reasonable, but do not expect top quality soil. Yet, the saving is worth the added work of improving what you get. Also check local newspaper classifieds; you might find a place that will let you take out soil for nothing if they happen to be excavating at the time. Or at least you will be able to buy the soil cheaply.

Before you add any soil to your property, however, have a soil test made so you will know what kind of soil you have and what you need to do to it. Such a test is a free service of either your State Agricultural Extension Service or your State Agricultural Experimental Station. (Who knows—you might be lucky and not have to add any new soil.) These organizations will tell you what kind of soil you have and recommend how to make it better. Dig up samples from a few spots in the garden. Take a few thin vertical slices from the side of the hole with a shovel. Mix the slices, and put a handful in a plastic bag and send it. A report will be returned to you in due time; it will tell you the pH of the soil, its texture, amounts of organic matter (phosporus and nitrogen), and what to do to improve your soil—a handy free guide that can save you labor and money. Valuable pamphlets offered by the U.S. Government Printing Service (see Chapter 6) include:

AB267	*Know Your Soil*, 1970 (free)
AB244	*Soil Conservation at Home*, 1969 (free)
M955	*Micro-organisms, What They Are*, 1964 (free)
AB320	*Know the Soil You Build On*, 1967 (free)
AB267	*Know Your Soil*, 1967 (free)
F2195	*Management of Sandy Soils in Central U.S.*, 1963 (free)
YB1957	*Soil* (Yearbook) 1957 ($4.00)

COMPOSTING

To improve your soil you will need humus (the stuff that makes a good soil). There is a simple way to make humus: composting. Humus is leaf mold and waste. There are always garden trimmings and kitchen waste to add to your existing soil to start your compost heap. You will also have to add nitrogen to transform the trash into rich compost. Manure, cottonseed meal, bone meal, blood meal, and even treated sewage sludge (which, by the way, is free for the asking) all contain the necessary nitrogen to get your compost pile transformed into rich humus.

To start your compost pile, use surplus green matter such as leaves, lawn clippings, and cuttings. Put in a little soil and some manure. (An ideal first layer is about 6 inches, but measuring is not necessary.) Manure is absolutely necessary; without it the compost will just sit and never decompose. You need the bacteria and fungi in the manure to

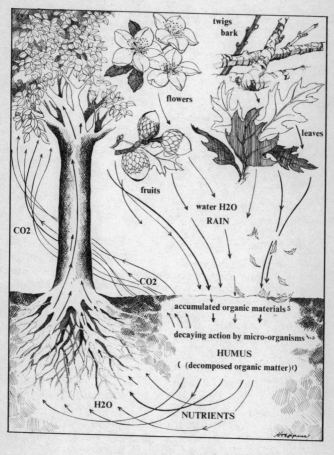

Nature's Compost System

30. Where did all the topsoil go? Stripped by the bulldozer and gone. Don't let this happen to you if you have a new home; have contractor pile soil in other areas for future use. (PHOTO BY AUTHOR)

transform the trash into valuable compost. (Do not add chemical additives because they can destroy the soil micro-organisms that do the work.) Over the manure, put in a thin bed of soil to hold in the heat. Then sprinkle some lime on top of the heap; this helps keep the compost from becoming too acidic. (Some plants like acid soils, but most do not.)

Air is needed in the compost pile so organisms can do their work. A simple method of ensuring air circulation is to place poles or pieces of wood in cross-hatch fashion at the bottom of the bin. Or simply drive stakes into the compost heap occasionally so air can gain entrance. Moisture is imperative.

Sprinkle water on the heap when necessary, but never allow the heap to get soggy or air circulation will be impeded. If it rains often in your area, make a roof to keep excess moisture from the compost. Mix and turn the compost frequently so that the heat in the center (which kills weed seeds) can work on all parts of the pile.

If you do not have enough compost for all your soil, stretch it by adding mulches. A booklet titled *Mulches For Your Garden*, 1970, G185, is available from the U.S. Government Printing Office. Some straw (sometimes free), lawn clippings (always free), or sawdust will do the trick. Remember that in the process of decay, nitrogen will be used up, so add nitrogen materials such as cottonseed meal or bone meal.

EARTHWORMS

To complete the garden soil picture, add earthworms. Yes, earthworms! These primitive animals grind up in their gizzards both mineral and organic matter that they then extrude as casings. Earthworms dig, grind, and combine ingredients and then return a rich porous soil. You can buy earthworms cheaply, or breed them even cheaper if they are not already in your soil.

Although the soil must have humus, it also requires good tilth (structure). Soil must be porous so air and water can enter it. Sawdust, which is free from lumber yards if you haul it yourself, is fine to help soil porosity. Indeed, when you buy soil conditioner at nurseries you are essentially buying a great deal of sawdust.

Make your own compost and you will have the beginnings of good soil without buying too much new

31. Earthworms do a world of good in soils; they aerate the soil and keep it porous. You can buy earthworms or raise your own. (PHOTO BY USDA)

earth. (See drawings for compost-bin construction and how to create your mound of money.) When the rich and crumbly black earth is ready for your garden (from 6 to 9 months), use it wisely. Put it on top, and hoe it lightly so the life process continues. Spread it over the garden, turning the old soil until it is crumbly and mixes with the new soil.

FERTILIZERS AND SOIL ADDITIVES

I am always amazed when I see the collection of fertilizers at local nurseries. What amazes me is the amount of money manufacturers earn for selling something you do not need if you garden intelligently.

Fertilizers are composed of nitrogen, phosphorus, and potassium; all these are available in organic rather than man-made materials. And chemical fertilizers may contain harmful by-products that can defeat your purpose. It is the organic matter that does the work. You can not add only fertilizer and have healthy plants; you need the organic matter to make living food for plants. Furthermore, the commercial fertilizer you buy is not all fertilizer; it is mostly filler.

Your local nursery carries a selection of soil additives, fertilizers, and gardening by-products (for want of a better name) that boggle the mind. Some are useful in the scheme of gardening, but most are not. Just because all these tidy little packages are on display does not mean that they will do anything more for your garden than you yourself can by other cheaper methods. Let us look at the many products in their pretty packages that tempt you to reach into your pocket.

Under fertilizers, there are a broad scope of man-made nitrogen-phosphorus-potash mishmashes. Percentages of each are marked on packages in the order given; for example: 10-10-5, 8-4-4, 0-10-10, and so forth. What do you really need for the garden? Well, if you have your own compost pile (and you should) and add it to soil regularly, you need very little else. In the last few years, organic gardeners have found this out and so rarely enter a nursery (and

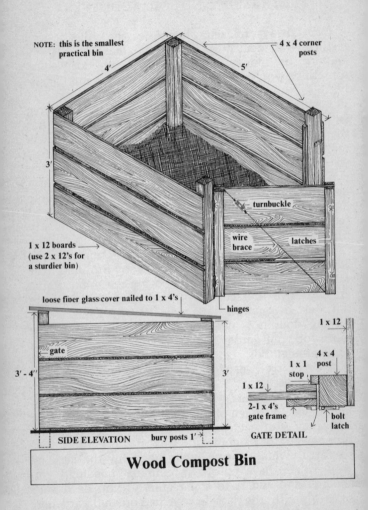

NOTE: this is the smallest practical bin

4'

5'

4 x 4 corner posts

3'

turnbuckle

wire brace

latches

1 x 12 boards (use 2 x 12's for a sturdier bin)

loose fiber glass cover nailed to 1 x 4's

hinges

gate

3' - 4"

3'

SIDE ELEVATION

bury posts 1'

1 x 12

4 x 4 post

1 x 1 stop

1 x 12

2-1 x 4's gate frame

bolt latch

GATE DETAIL

Wood Compost Bin

156

32. Soil should be crumbly and black, as shown, never caked and gray. (USDA PHOTO)

33. Composting is easy and makes good humus for soil so plants grow well. Start your own compost pile and beat the cost of soil. (USDA PHOTO)

34. Leaves stored in wire containers make fine fodder for the compost bin. (USDA PHOTO)

they really do not have to). You can do the same, even if you are not a bonafide organic devotee.

In addition to the standard fertilizers mentioned above, there are specific plant foods for roses, citrus, and azaleas. The manufacturer's premise is that if you have a favorite plant, you will be more prone to spend money on it. The decision of course is yours, but thousands of us have grown roses and azaleas for years without tons of additives and with considerable success. Testimonials are not necessary. Simply pick up a copy of the fine magazine *Organic Gardening*, or better yet, subscribe to it for up-to-the-minute hints and tips on organic gardening. Also, there are two free brochures on fertilizing available from the U.S. Printing Office:

L307   *How Much Fertilizer Should I Use,*
       1963
G89   *Selecting Fertilizers for Lawn and*
       Garden, 1971

If you think the manufacturers have stopped at plant foods, take another look. At your nursery you will find aluminum sulfate, ammonia sulfate, iron sulfate, sulfate of potash, and even charcoal in packages. There seems to be no end to the things you can buy to make your garden grow. Each has, according to the manufacturer, something to make a plant grow better or to remedy a plant ailment. I have never used any of these materials, and my four gardens prosper and have been featured in national magazines. And even if you did need some of these additives for your plants, there are free sources to get them; for example, charcoal from any old fireplace or lime from many by-products.

This brings us to the organic materials sold at suppliers. These include such valuable soil additives as

Substance	Nitrogen, %	Phosphorus, %	Potassium, %
*Hoof and horn meal	13		
*Blood meal	13		
Fish meals	9-14	3 or more	
*Bone meal	3		
*Cottonseed meal	7	1.1	1.36
†Castor pomace	6		
Buckwheat middlings	4.75	1	1
†Meat and bone scraps	8	5	
†Sunflower-seed oil cake	5.5	1	1
*Dry steer and cow manure	2		
†Wood ashes			2.5-5
†Alfalfa hay	2.35	0.21	2

*Available in sacks at nurseries.
†Free in some areas.

steer manure, cottonseed meal, blood meal (very expensive), peat moss, hoof and horn meal, and leaf mold. If you are in a farming area, you will probably be able to get manure for nothing, but fresh manure can be dangerous for plants and burn them. So because of availability and odor, you will do best to buy manures in tidy packages. Cottonseed meal and blood meal are two costly essentials of good gardening that return their worth. These are sometimes available through farm stores at reasonable prices if you live in rural areas; otherwise you will just have to pay the price. Leaf mold in packages is costly too, so if you know people with property, beg, borrow and ask to steal it. I have several friends who allow me to take some humus from their land. In time, nature replenishes the humus in the forest, and in the meantime you have some for your garden without spending a cent.

As mentioned, if you keep the compost pile going, you can take advantage of free earth without harming the ecology one bit. In fact, you will be helping things along by getting rid of wastes by returning them to nature. So other than a few sacks of blood or cottonseed meal, let nature do the rest, and leave your pocketbook intact!

On the opposite page is a table of some organic substances. They may cost money, but they have no fillers, so there are no added elements to pay for.

DRAINAGE MATERIALS

Drainage materials (gravel, for example) cost money. Look for free sources if you can because if you want healthy plants (and who doesn't) you are going to need some drainage materials so excess water can drain from the soil. Otherwise, the bottom of the soil becomes a soggy mess that turns sour and then turns plants roots sour. Soil must have air passages so water, nutrients, and air can circulate. Gravel or crushed rock has many surfaces, so water is distributed, drains away, and evaporates. But because gravel and crushed stone cost money, try other porous materials such as crushed brick, broken pot pieces, and even crushed glass.

Broken bricks are free at sites where buildings have been wrecked. Generally, if you ask, you can have them. (Whole ones can be used for garden paths, but you will not find many bricks intact). Crack the broken bricks with a hammer for a fine source of drainage material. Use discarded broken terra cotta clay pots as another good substitute for gravel. You can get broken glass at local glass stores, usually for nothing if you take it away. These cut-off pieces can be crushed, and make an excellent source of drainage material.

INSECT CONTROL

As a nation we are fully aware of the harm done to the earth by chemicals. Yet, invariably, bugs may enter our garden, so what to do? First do not make the manufacturer rich by buying dubious chemicals (not only will you deplete your pocketbook, you will be depleting the earth of birds and beneficial insects). There are other less expensive and, in most cases, free ways of fighting the bugs.

Beneficial insects—ladybugs and wasps—and birds are your first line of defense. There are also other methods to keep bugs from the garden; they may be old fashioned, but they are almost free. Handpicking

35. Gravel will ensure good drainage in soil. If it is too costly, use broken bricks, pot shards or any type material that has many-faceted surfaces so water can flow freely and evaporate. (PHOTO BY AUTHOR)

is one way, unpleasant though it may be. However, a
better and more effective way is simply to use a
laundry soap-and-water solution. A 1-pound bar of
laundry soap costs about 19 cents and will make
gallons of repellent. Dissolve half the bar in a little
boiling water, and add about 2 gallons of water to
make an excellent insect spray. Mist or douse plants
and you will have better protection than you would
with all the costly insecticides—and you will not harm
the environment.

Sticky band (sometimes sold as Tanglefoot) is
another good, and inexpensive preventative. You can

36. The praying mantis is a veritable insect-eating machine. They can be purchased inexpensively from suppliers.

37. Ladybugs are well known for their voracious appetite for aphids. Never kill them for they will patrol and keep your garden plants free from aphids.

make your own from equal parts of pine tar and molasses.

Milk cartons slipped around young plants and buried a little in the soil will discourage many insects. Cutworms, for example, will not be able to scale the waxed walls; ordinary roofing paper will do if you run out of milk cartons. A Coleman lantern mounted above a pail of water with a float of kerosene will attract moths and various harmful insects: once enticed by the light they will fall to their death in the oil.

You can also make your own nicotine solutions by letting tobacco steep in water for a few days. Use 1 pound to 4 gallons of water. This concoction is highly effective in eliminating aphids, thrips, and leafhoppers. It can be sprayed or dumped into soil. For soil mealybugs (becoming increasingly prevalant), bury some old pipe tobacco or cigarette tobacco at the site of infestation, and water thoroughly. The nicotine will leach through the soil to destroy the pests.

Solutions made from plants and used as natural preventatives are another way to eliminate insects. For those who would like to have free insecticides on the property, grow *Chrysanthemum cinerariaefolium*. (The name alone is enough to scare off bugs!) You can get the seed from England via Thompson & Morgan or from some seed specialists here. The plant needs warmth and plenty of moisture. Seep the flower petals in boiling water to make a solution. Then add more water and douse plants and soil.

Rotenone is another good substance to use to thwart insects. It is contained in the roots of several tropical plants. In the United States the weed called "devils shoestring" contains rotenone. Dry and pulverize the plant to secure the insecticide, and then mix it with some water.

Hellebore is another plant that contains an insect repellent. Mix the powder from it with ordinary limestone and sift it around plants. You can also buy wood chips of Quassia for a small price. Soak 1 pound of the chips in 10 gallons of water and use as a spray.

These solutions from plants are equal to or better than commercial ones, at one-hundredth the cost. All you need are the above-mentioned plants. Some U.S. Government Printing Office Publications about pest control are:

F2148	*Aphids on Leaf Vegetables*, 1969
G46	*Insects and Disease of Vegetables in the Home Garden*, 1971
PA725	*For a Beautiful America Guard Against Plant Pests*, 1969

(Some of these pamphlets prescribe insecticide usage, so read with a careful eye.)

BENEFICIAL INSECTS FOR BIOLOGICAL CONTROL

Bio-Control Co.
Rt. 2, P.O. Box 2397
Auburn, California 95603

Ladybug beetles; sometimes mantis cases

Ecological Insect Services
15075 W. California Ave.
Kerman, California 93630

Gothard, Inc.
P.O. Box 370
Canutillo, Texas 79835

Trichogramma wasps

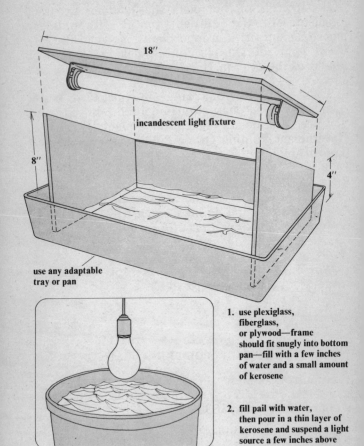

18''

incandescent light fixture

8''

4''

use any adaptable
tray or pan

1. use plexiglass,
   fiberglass,
   or plywood—frame
   should fit snugly into bottom
   pan—fill with a few inches
   of water and a small amount
   of kerosene

2. fill pail with water,
   then pour in a thin layer of
   kerosene and suspend a light
   source a few inches above

168

Mincemoyer's Nursery R.D. 5, P.O. Box 379 New Prospect Rd. Jackson, New Jersey 08527	Mantis egg cases
Schoor's Sierra Bug Co. P.O. Box 114 Rough and Ready, California 95975	Ladybugs only
The Vitova Co., Inc. Biological Control Division P.O. Box 745 Rialto, California 92376	Lacewings; two kinds of trichogramma
World Garden Products 2 First St. East Norwalk, Connecticut 06855	Ladybugs

TRAPS FOR INSECTS

Agrilite Systems, Inc.
404 Barringer Bldg.
Columbia, South Carolina 29201

Ray Collier
2499 Greenway St. South
St. Petersburg, Florida 33712

D-vac Co.
P.O. Box 2095
Riverside, California 92506

Electro-Lite Dist. Co.
Dept. 3B
12507-11 Ave. N.
Minneapolis, Minnesota 55427

Insect-O-Lite Company
1925 Queen City Ave.
Cincinnati, Ohio 45214

The Tanglefoot Company
314 Straight Ave., S.W.
Grand Rapids, Michigan 49500

HERBS AND BOTANICAL REPELLENTS

Greene Herb Gardens
Greene, Rhode Island 02827

Indiana Botanic Gardens, Inc.
Hammond, Indiana 46325

Merry Gardens
Camden, Maine 04843

Nichols Garden Nursery
1190 Pacific Hwy.
Albany, Oregon 97321

Pine Hill Herb Farms
P.O. Box 114
Rosewell, Georgia 30075

Sunnybrook Farms Nursery
9448 Mayfield Rd.
Chesterland, Ohio 44026

NATURAL INSECTICIDES

Agra Industries, Ltd.
355 Lexington Ave.
New York, New York 10017

Chemical Compounding Co.
1459 Third St.
Oakland, California 94607

McLaughlin Gormley King Co.
1715 5th Street, S.E.
Minneapolis, Minnesota 55414

Pyrethrum Information Center
Room 423
744 Broad St.
Newark, New Jersey 07102

Thompson & Morgan
London Road
Ipswich-Suffolk
England

EARTHWORMS

Brazos Worm Farm
Route 9
Waco, Texas 76705

Oakhaven Enterprises
Cedar Hills, Texas 75104

Andrew Peoples
R.D. #1
Lansdale, Pennsylvania 19445

Sunada Enterprises
P.O. Box 362
Parlier, California 93648

THE MOST POPULAR AND BESTSELLING NON-FICTION FROM PINNACLE BOOKS

BURN AFTER READING, by Ladislas Farago. Here are the spymasters, the heroes, the traitors, and all the cryptic subtlety and horrific violence that marked their grim activities. The more gripping because it really happened—it's all fascinating, particularly if you bear in mind that the same sort of thing is going on right this minute, as clandestinely and just as ruthlessly. By the author of GAME OF THE FOXES and PATTON. Fast-moving, smoothly written, yet fully documented.

P090--95¢

THE CANARIS CONSPIRACY, by Roger Manvell and Heinrich Fraenkel. An astounding chronicle of the plot to kill Hitler. This is the documented story of the work of Admiral Wilhelm Canaris' Department Z, pieced together from the accounts of survivors and told in full for the first time. This group attempted to liquidate Hitler in order to make peace with the allies, but before the plotters could achieve their goal, the conspiracy was discovered and broken by arrests, executions and suicides. One of the most incredible stories to come out of World War II.

P093–$1.25

DIVINE THUNDER, by Bernard Millot. This is the story of the kamikazes, the suicide pilots of Japan during World War II, and of why, when the need arose, they were ready to die without hesitation. In both soldiers and civilians, a mystical reverence for the homeland was almost second nature. The author describes their devastating assaults and the American reaction to them and he reveals what made the kamikazes men of such strange grandeur and heroism. With original drawings.

P108–$1.25

THE KENNEDY WOMEN, by Pearl S. Buck. Here are the fascinating and extraordinary women of the Kennedy family. With the skill of a journalist, the artistry of a gifted storyteller, and the seasoned eye of a biographer, Pearl S. Buck paints a portrait in words of the women who bear one of the most famous family names in history. From Rose, the durable and dynamic matriarch, to JFK's young Caroline—and including Kathleen, Rosemary, Patricia, Jean, Eunice, Ethel, Joan and Jacqueline—these are the ladies of our times.

P113–$1.50

STAND BY TO DIE, by A. V. Sellwood. The heroic story of a lone, embattled WW II ship. It was a small Yangtse river steamer, manned by a makeshift crew of fugitives. She sailed from war-torn Singapore to do battle with the armed might of a Japanese fleet. It was an epic naval action. Heroism was the order of the day. There were no lean British cruisers to divert the Japanese guns, there were no RAF planes to provide air cover. Just one bullet-riddled tub that wouldn't say die! The story could have been lost forever, as it has been for many years, had not A. V. Sellwood pieced together the almost unbelievable story of "the most decorated small ship in the navy."

P171--95¢

SIEGE AND SURVIVAL: THE ODYSSEY OF A LENINGRADER. by Elena Skrjabina. A diary of one of the most devastating sieges in history. During the siege of Leningrad which began on September 8, 1941, nearly one-and-one-half million people died—of hunger, of cold, of disease, from German bullets and bombs. Elena Skrjabina survived. She endured. This book is a record of that experience, and it has been acclaimed by critics everywhere. *Publishers Weekly* said that it is "written in unadorned but eloquent prose that is remarkably effecting." *Bestsellers* said "It is human."

P199--95¢

VIZZINI!, by Sal Vizzini, with Oscar Fraley and Marshall Smith. The secret lives of our most successful narc! Sal Vizzini may die because he wrote this book. He was formerly an undercover agent for the Federal Bureau of Narcotics—an assignment which took him to Naples, where he became a "friend" of exiled Mafia chieftain Charles "Lucky" Luciano; to Burma, where he blew up a heroin factory; to Lebanon, where he outwitted a Communist gun-running ring; and to Atlanta, Georgia, where he posed as a con in the Federal pen. He was shot three times, knifed twice, beaten nearly to death, and had several contracts put out by the Mafia to kill him. Many of the men now in jail will learn for the first time who put them there.

P226-$1.25

WALKING TALL, by Doug Warren. The true story of Buford Pusser a sheriff who has become a living legend. Buford is an honest man, a good man, he has tried to clean out the criminal element of his community. In doing so he has been shot eight times, stabbed five, rammed by a speeding car, had his home fire bombed, and was trapped in an ambush that killed his wife. But, Buford still lives. He raided the prostitution houses, the gambling dens and illicit moonshine stills and almost single handedly ousted crooked officials. His story has been made into a major motion picture by Cinerama.

P478-$1.25

BUGSY, by George Carpozi, Jr. The wild but true story of Benjamin "Bugsy" Siegel. By the time he was twenty-one, this handsome hoodlum had done almost everything a professional mobster could do. It was Bugsy Siegel who transformed a sandy wasteland into Las Vegas. The same Bugsy Siegel who hobnobbed with Hollywood's royalty and was treated almost as a king himself. He traveled widely, ate in the finest restaurants, and owned an estate in Beverly Hills. His women were legion. But never far beneath the surface was a hard-eyed killer—a killer who died as violently as he lived.   P244—$1.25

MICKEY COHEN: MOBSTER, by Ed Reid. Finally—the brutal truth about a well-known gangster! This is a story that Mickey Cohen would rather *not* have told, but a story that can no longer be kept secret. Mickey Cohen is a man who has always been larger than life, who is part of the social history of our time. He's a member of the Jewish Mafia, who has lived hard and lived flamboyantly; who brags about deeds most would want hidden; whose friends have been jet-setters, criminals, evangelists, film stars, politicians, and members of the Hollywood social scene. Right now, he's down but not out, and don't ever count him *out*! Not until the end.   P257—$1.25

SUSAN HAYWARD: THE DIVINE BITCH, by Doug McClelland. The triumphs and tragedies of a fiery and talented screen star. Susan Hayward has lived a life to pale even her most vivid screen roles. There were two marriages, twin sons, and constant strife that persists to this day. She was a feminist before the fashion—with femininity plus and a drive to achieve that led her far from the Brooklyn tenement where she began her life. This is the first book ever on one of the First Ladies of the movies' Golden Age: Susan Hayward.   P276—$1.25

INSIDE ADOLF HITLER, by Roger Manvell and Heinrich Fraenkel. This is *not* a book about politics. It is *not* a book about warfare. What is it then? It is a book about the mind of a man, a probing portrait into the personality development of the most hated man of the 20th century. **INSIDE ADOLF HITLER** is by two of the most renowned Third Reich historians. Their most recent books, *The Canaris Conspiracy* and *The Men Who Tried To Kill Hitler*, have sold millions. Here, for the first time, is an in-depth analysis of the public and private personalities of Adolf Hitler.   P277—$1.50

Sex, sociology & marriage books everyone is buying

THE TRUE CONFESSIONS AND WILD ADVENTURES OF TWO RENT-A-GIRLS, by Julie Nelson and Linda Tracey. The inside story of beautiful girls for hire! Meet the Rent-a-Girls—Julie and Linda—two gorgeous young ladies who are ready and willing to provide entertainment and companionship for any man who can afford the price. Rent-a-Girls is the most exciting service organization ever devised. They tell you everything from how to hire a Rent-a-Girl to how to become a Rent-a-Girl—all the rules, the do's and don'ts. **P269—$1.25**

THE CIVILIZED COUPLE'S GUIDE TO EXTRA-MARITAL ADVENTURE, by Dr. Alber Ellis Psychotherapist, authority on sex and author of thirty books including *Sex Without Guilt*, has again broken ground in the understanding of male-female relationships. In this book, he shows that the need to have an affair is quite the norm and shows how to go about it with a maximum of pleasure and a minimum of guilt and embarrassment. And for those who are unsatisfied in their marriages but disinclined to have an affair, Dr. Ellis has also included a chapter on how to be both happy and monogamous.

P273—$1.25

THE MATING TRADE, by John Godwin. The mating trade is a billion-dollar industry that is growing by leaps and bounds. John Godwin, under an assumed name, set out to discover why. He joined matchmaking organizations—lonely hearts clubs, key clubs, singles bars, cruise ships, resorts, swingles apartments, and encounter groups. He interviewed over two hundred people—entrepreneurs in the new business, employees, and the clients themselves. Ready and eager to talk about their sex lives, people gave him information that was startling in the extreme. All this makes for an easy-to-read, entertaining, yet most informative book. **P290—$1.25**

A SLIGHTLY USED WOMAN, by Peter Kortner. The one story Hollywood has not dared to tell! This is a work of fiction based upon truth. For Carol Sutton, the fading film star who is trying to make a comeback in a TV series, does exist. She must make a choice between three men—one, a producer who can promise her wealth; the second, her former husband, who is determined to win her back; and the third, a handsome black man, whom she employs as a houseboy. She needs the series, her agent needs the success and the money, the sponsor needs a prestige deal. **P296—$1.25**

SWINGER'S DIARY, by Iris Brent. A daringly intimate revelation of the swinging life, authored by a couple who participated in the super-sensual world of group-sex. Iris Brent and her husband emerge as real people with real feelings and real concerns about what might happen to their marriage, children and careers if they stepped out of the so-called normal bounds of contemporary morality. But they did it and they joined the swinging society in earnest. Here is their story as swingers—and how it affected their lives. **P181—$1.25**

THE PHALLIC MYSTIQUE, by G. L. Simmons. An entertaining study of a long-taboo subject! Maybe Freud was wrong, and all women don't want one, but they are certainly curious about them. And most men, happy as they may be with their endowment, have questions. Some they are embarrassed to ask, some they are afraid to ask. Here are the answers, in a breakthrough book based on extensive research; a book that is fun to read, informative, and controversial at the same time. **P217—$95¢**

THE SEX CLINIC, by J. J. Lily. The inside story of an institute for sexual therapy—and the exciting woman who knew what every man needed. The institute was developed to treat men who had lost all capacity for sexual activity. They used sympathetic, sexually experienced women capable of restoring confidence and guiding the patient toward a healthy sexual life. This is the story of one woman's work at the institute, told in her own words—the story of the men who came there, of the effect that working there had on her, and ultimately, the story of the clinic itself.

P231—95¢

INSIDE LINDA LOVELACE, by Linda Lovelace. Finally, the book you've been hearing about! Here is the exclusive and incredible story—for the first time anywhere, the *true* story—of Linda Lovelace, star of the most controversial sex-film of this decade. There will be a centerfold pinup; new, revealing and never-before-published pictures of Linda; exciting, behind-the-scenes stories from the making of *Deep Throat*. The secrets of Linda's life, loves, sexual techniques and unusual talents. **P240—$1.75**

YOUR SEX DRIVE, by Robert Chartham, Ph.D. A fascinating study of the urge to make love. Dr. Robert Chartham, author of the bestselling books, *The Sensuous Couple* and *Your Sexual Future,* has again broken a new barrier in the understanding of the sexual urge, known as the drive to make love. Dr. Chartham is both a scientist and a skilled writer, adept at explaining and illuminating those areas so long kept in the dark.
P087 $1.25

HOW TO "MAKE IT" 365 DAYS A YEAR, by Paul Warren. Turn on *all* of your senses! Tune in to the sensitivities of the species. Every male has the sensual potentials—and equipment. But not every male has learned or practiced the most effective ways to make use of his sexual powers. And that's where it's at, man. Ask any woman.
This book is designed as a short course—a crash program, if necessary—in sensuality. It is required reading for every man interested in women.
For the uninitiated beginner *or* the self-styled super-lover there's much to be discovered in these pages.   **P092 $1.25**

THE WOMAN LOVER, by Rick Davish. An erotic, satirical, very funny book, reminiscent of *Portnoy's Complaint.* Abramovich, the central figure, is sometimes comic, sometimes tragic—but always aroused. He's looking for an answer to the questions of life—searching for his soul—but is invariably diverted by his sex urges. No nice Jewish man would act this way, so he tries Yoga, a Baptist church (black), group therapy, his synagogue, and active sports. There is only one sport he really likes. Will our hero free himself of his obsession? Will he fight successfully his desire to put his †††††††††††††††† into as many ********** as he can locate? Will he overcome his need to ‡‡‡‡‡‡‡‡‡‡‡? Read THE WOMAN LOVER to find out.
P123 $1.25

THE COLLEGE SEX LIFE LETTERS edited by Jay David. What's really happening under the covers in today's colleges? In response to an advertisement placed in campus newspapers around the nation, college students have frankly and anonymously responded with letters detailing their current sexual activities and proclivities. The uninhibited and explicit responses of the students whose letters are contained in this candid collection will give the reader a new awareness of the pleasure, joys, fantasies and perversions which are being practiced as the new campus morality. P424 $1.50

SEXUAL MARATHON, by Martin Shepard & Marjorie Lee. Take eight people—four men and four women—remove all their clothes and their sexual inhibitions. That's the beginning of a sexual marathon. The eight people chosen for this experiment in emotional exchange are all quite different in their ideas about sex. This is an eye-witness report of every word, sound and action in a most revealing new experiment in sexual analysis.   **P150—$1.25**

SEXUAL CYBERNETICS, by Dr. Paul Gillette. Sexual cybernetics is a trail-blazing system for the individual who wants to control his sexual responses; to take full command of his sex life; to learn to build satisfying sexual relationships; to increase and channel sexual energies!
SEXUAL CYBERNETICS, written for the layman, by an eminent psychologist and sexologist.
This is the indispensable guide for those who want to master their sexual powers, and control those of others; the indispensable guide to sexual satisfaction.   **P159—$1.25**

EROTIC FANTASIES OF WOMEN, by Marjorie Lee. A candid analysis of the waking dreams of normal women! Here, for the first time, the intimate desires of women are explored with sensitivity and honesty. Twenty-four average American women, representing all levels of society were chosen as subjects. These are not swingers Ms. Lee is writing about—but rather those women who would not dare to act out their erotic fantasies. They have consented to reveal their innermost longings to the author—a prominent sexologist—with the understanding that they will remain anonymous.   **P174—$1.50**

THE LOVE GAME, by Bill and Judy. An exciting and sexy new book that's really a game. It looks like a book. It feels like a book. And it's for sale where paperback books are sold. But it is a game. You open it, and play with it. All that's needed are a man and a woman (preferably interested in each other). From the first, gentle beginnings with love talk, to the exciting, climactic finale, the pages of this book act as instructional guide. By combining verbal and physical communication, lovers can reach new heights in excitement while finding new depths in their loving relationship.
          P175—$2.95

Sex, sociology & marriage books everyone is buying

HOW TO MARRY A MARRIED MAN, by Mary Eng
This is a guide for the single woman who has found
man, but found him already married; to his wife, his ca
his past or even his hobby. The directions are practical
straightforward, and buttressed with case histories
illustrate each problem and *his* solution. It has been wri
for the healthy and attractive woman who wants to
married or remarried to a man who is already commit
P057—

THE GROUPSEX SCENE, by John F. Trimble, Ph.D.
new, shocking and intimate account reveals what Group
is all about and how it may affect our society even y
GroupSex helps answer questions as the author introdu
you to this very controversial subject through the exp
ences of a young married couple. It is this couple who
what it is like to engage in GroupSex its pros and its co
Whether the idea disgusts you or intrigues you, it i
lifestyle that is here.   P058—$1

**PURR, BABY, PURR, by Lucianne Goldberg and Jear
Sakol.** An honest, pertinent, funny but feminine reply
Women's Lib, which sets out the principles of the Pu
cats, a league of women who believe in femininity,
feminism. They're proud to be women. They believe 1
reform is better achieved through persuasion; not marc
yelling, kicking or threatening. Pussycats believe in pam
ing men; you can guess whose side the men are on!
P068—$1

Great exercise self-help books from Pinnacle!

STAY YOUNG WITH ASTROLOGY, by Frank J. McCarthy. Now for the first time a renowned astrologer reveals the formula for lasting youth hidden in YOUR own Sun Sign. Every Sign of the Zodiac has its own special youth-giving secrets. Now, revealed for you—whatever your Sign is the way to remain full of life no matter what calendar age you reach. It has long been known and accepted that the stars have an incredible influence on the kind of person you are—but what is little known is that they can help you to enjoy a healthy, youthful, sex-filled life right through your golden years.   **PO16 95¢**

RELAXERCISES, by Joan Frazer. The rhythmic way to a healthier, prettier figure, designed especially for women. A system of exercise that is as easy as it is refreshing and effective. No woman alive wants to grow old—or look old. With these exercises any woman can subtract years—and feel younger, too. Relaxercising is a method based on proven principles of natural body movements. Here's the new way to begin remodeling the figure, shaping the back, whittling the waist, trimming legs and hips, developing the bosom, releasing nervous tensions, prettyfying the face, and much more.   **PO88 $1.25**

EXECUTIVE YOGA, by Harvey Day. Never has there been a more urgent need for Yoga—especially for tired, fast-paced businessmen who daily face stresses for which their bodies are not prepared. Never was there a more urgent need for men to know how to relax; to breathe, exercise, eat, drink and care for their bodies. In this comprehensive and well-illustrated book, Harvey Day accomplishes these tasks and more. He shows that character, too, is important to the effective businessman, and how Yogis for over 6000 years have developed a working philosophy.   **PO98 $1.25**

MASSAGE: THE LOVING TOUCH, by Stephen Lewis. A guide to the subtle and sensual art of massage. Touching. For years it was a subject to be ignored in our society. Suddenly it's very much talked about—an important means of communication in our impersonal world. And that's what massage is. Touching. For therapy, for sensual communication, for relaxation, for warmth. It can be a health aid, a way to learn about your own body and how it reacts. In this superbly illustrated book, Stephen Lewis shows the reader how to massage and tells him why to massage. He teaches him how to touch. **P135—$1.95**

This is your Order Form . . .
Just clip and mail.

_____	P090	BURN AFTER READING, Ladislas Farago	.95
_____	P093	THE CANARIS CONSPIRACY, Manvell & Fraenkel	1.25
_____	P108	DIVINE THUNDER, Bernard Millot	1.25
_____	P113	THE KENNEDY WOMEN, Pearl S. Buck	1.50
_____	P171	STAND BY TO DIE, A. V. Sellwood	.95
_____	P199	SIEGE & SURVIVAL, Elena Skrjabina	.95
_____	P226	VIZZINI, Sal Vizzini, with Fraley & Smith	1.25
_____	P478	WALKING TALL, Doug Warren	$1.25
_____	P244	BUGSY, George Carpozi, Jr.	1.25
_____	P257	MICKEY COHEN: MOBSTER, Ed Reid	1.25
_____	P276	SUSAN HAYWARD: THE DIVINE BITCH, Doug McClelland	1.25
_____	P277	INSIDE ADOLF HITLER, Manvell & Fraenkel	1.50

TO ORDER

Please check the space next to the book/s you want, send this order form together with your check or money order, include the price of the book/s and 25¢ for handling and mailing, to:

PINNACLE BOOKS, INC. / P.O. Box 4347,
Grand Central Station / New York, N.Y. 10017

☐ CHECK HERE IF YOU WANT A FREE CATALOG.

I have enclosed $_____check_____or money order_____
as payment in full. No C.O.D.'s.

Name_____

Address_____

City_____State_____Zip_____
(Please allow time for delivery.)